AWAKENING

HEALTHY FOOD

FOR THE

BODY AND SOUL

Mary Brickell

I would like to dedicate this book to the wonderful family God has given me. I love them very much, and all of them have been a loving support to me throughout the years.

I would like to thank my daughter-in-law for all the time she spent helping me to proofread this book. Also, thanks to my son-in-law Chris, granddaughter Tabitha, and husband Gary for helping me to complete my book cover.

INTRODUCTION

After 50 years as a ladies' Bible study teacher, God inspired me to write these devotional studies because of my passion for making His word known. God's word has amazing power to change our lives more than our words alone could ever accomplish. In Hebrews 4:12, it says, "The word of God is alive and active, sharper than any double-edged sword, it penetrates even to dividing soul and spirit, joints, and marrow, and it judges the thoughts and attitudes of the heart." It also says in Isaiah 55:11, "God's word will not come back to Him empty but will accomplish what He desires and will achieve the purpose for which it was sent." When considering these verses, they conveyed to me the importance of writing each devotional study backed up with other scripture, which ended up being more like a Bible study. You can do each one as a devotional or take the time you need to meditate on all the scripture from each devotional to do a Bible study. Hopefully, these devotional studies will give you a deeper understanding of God and His word. In Psalms 34:8 it says, "taste and see that that the Lord is Good", so I pray these studies will give you a taste of how good God's word is so you will have the desire to be in His word daily!

My other passion has been to help people with their physical health so they can experience a better quality of life. I've used that passion in my Natural Health Care practice for over 27 years. I've worked at Health Food Stores, had an online Health Food Store, and for eight years owned and operated a Health Food Store. Then I opened a clinic in my home after my retirement from the store.

In I Corinthians 6:19, it tells us that the body is the temple of the Holy Spirit. God has given each of us an amazing body that can heal itself when it has the nutrients it needs. As Christians, we especially should respect our bodies as a Holy Temple and make better choices in eating and taking care of our bodies. Hopefully, the health tips in this book will give you more insight into how the body works and your part to assist in keeping it healthy.

My husband suggested including my healthy recipes in the book, too. So, I decided to combine both of my passions by writing a devotional study with a related health tip and healthy recipes at the back of the book. My prayer is that you will feed your body and soul each day with healthy food for the abundant life it speaks of in John 10:10, which God wants for us.

TABLE OF CONTENTS

AWAKENING

HEALTHY FOOD
FOR THE
BODY AND SOUL

Mary Brickell

KNOWING GOD

"God is not a man that He would lie, or a human being that He would change His mind. Has He ever spoken and not done it, or promised and not fulfilled it?"

Numbers 23:19

How much do we really know about God? In the Bible, the book of Genesis says He is the creator of everything. Although, as humans, we have limited understanding, it is almost impossible to fully comprehend who God is. He is Spirit, which means that He doesn't have a body, so He is invisible, immortal, and eternal.[1] Even though we cannot see God, He is revealed to us throughout the Bible by His characteristics. These characteristics give us faith to put our hope in Him.

Infinite - "I Am the Alpha and the Omega." (Revelation 1:8 NAS). God's self-existence is one of the most difficult characteristics of God to understand. God, as creator alone, is worthy of our praise (Revelation 4:11).

Immutable - God never changes, so you can trust His character, and words will never change (Psalm 102:25-27, Hebrews 13:8). This should be a source of incredible joy for believers in a changing world!

---

[1] John 4:24, I Timothy 1:17

Self-Sufficient - God has no needs because He was not created but the creator (Psalm 24:1). This means there is nothing you can give Him that He wants but your heart (Luke 10:27).

Omnipotent - The Bible is clear that God is all-powerful and can do anything (Jeremiah 32:17, I Chronicles 29:11). His great power can accomplish much in your life if you allow Him to (Ephesians 1:18-19).

Omniscient - He has complete knowledge of everything (Hebrews 4:13). He is the only one who knows everything we are going to say and do. He even knew us before we were born (Psalm 139:4,13-16).

Omnipresent - God is everywhere all the time (Psalm 139:7-12). It is a comfort to know that God is with you always, so you do not need to be afraid (Isaiah 41:10, Hebrews 13:5).

Wise - God made everything from His great wisdom (Psalm 104:24). He promises to give us wisdom if we ask (James 1:5).

Faithful - God is faithful all the time, even when we are not (II Timothy 2:13). You can hold fast to the assurance of your salvation because He is faithful (Hebrews 10:23).

Good - Since God is good, He will do only good for you and work bad into good (James 1:17, Romans 8:28).

Just - He uses the purest standards as a fair judge and knows the true intentions of each person to show justice accordingly (Proverbs 21:2). God is Just with salvation since He gives everyone a chance to receive Him (II Peter 3:9).

Merciful - God's mercy is rooted in love for His people to show them compassion. Without the mercy of God, we would have no hope of Heaven (Ephesians 2:4-5). His mercies toward us are new every day (Lamentations 3:22-23).

Gracious - God showed undeserved favor in salvation (Ephesians 2:8-9). His grace is sufficient in our weakness in times of need (II Corinthians 12:9).

Loving - God's love is a sacrificial love (John 3:16), calls us His children (John 1:12-13), and will complete the work He has started in us (Philippians 1:6).

Holy - God is set apart from any evil. So, when we sin, it places a distance in our relationship until we confess it (I John 1:9).

Glorious - God is majestic in all His splendor and beauty, and we only see a bit of that in His creation now (Ezekiel 1:26-28).

When we know God's character, it will help us understand how that applies to our lives and how He works in the world. This knowledge can strengthen our trust in God so we do not lean on our own understanding, and we can truly Praise Him for who He is![2]

---

[2] Proverbs 3:5-6, Hebrews 13:14-15

UNDERSTANDING BRAIN HEALTH

We can know God because He has given us a brain to think and communicate with Him. God created this amazing, intricate brain to help our whole body to function. The brain is one of the largest and most complex organs in the human body. It consist of more than one hundred billion nerves that communicate in trillions of connections. The brain controls our breathing, sleep, coordination, balance, sensations, handwriting, body positions, memory, hearing, and eyesight, just to name a few. Since your body can not function without your brain, we should take exceptional care of it. Here are some helpful tips for a healthy brain:

Exercise regularly - Exercise is known to have good benefits for our body, but physical activity also benefits the brain. Research studies have shown that people who are physically active are less likely to experience a decline in their mental function and have a lower risk of developing Alzheimer's disease. The benefits are a result of increased blood flow to your brain during exercise. It can also alter the natural reduction in brain connections that occur during aging, plus reversing some of the health concerns. You can walk, swim, play tennis, or any other moderate activity that increases your heart rate. Low-impact exercise is usually the most effective form of exercise and of those exercises, walking has been considered the most effective.

Get plenty of sleep - Sleep plays a key role in your brain health. Most people need seven to eight consecutive hours of sleep per night. Consecutive sleep gives your brain the time to consolidate and store your memories effectively. Seniors usually have a more challenging time sleeping due to different health conditions.

Eat a healthy diet - Your diet plays a key role in your brain health. Your diet should consist of mainly plant-based food, which is easier to digest. Also, whole grains, substantial amounts of dark green leafy vegetables, a variety of fruits, and healthy fats are also good. Stay away from refined sugars, refined flour, animal fats, hydrogenated oils, and processed food. People who follow this diet are less likely to have Alzheimer's. Supplements that are good for brain health are Fish Oils with higher amounts of DHA, Vitamin B100 complex, plus extra B6, Vitamin D drops, Magnesium, and Gingko Biloba.

Stay mentally active - Your brain is like a muscle that you need to use, or you lose it. It is also important to stimulate right to left brain connections. You can stand up to do leg lifts, in which you bend one knee at a time and touch the opposite elbow to each knee. I do this exercise every day and find it helpful for my memory. That is just one idea but there are more exercises you can do specifically for brain health, which you can Google to find. There are many activities that you can do to keep your brain in shape, such as doing crossword puzzles, reading, playing cards, or putting together a jigsaw puzzle. Consider it cross-training for your brain. So, it is important to incorporate different activities to increase the effectiveness of your brain.

Remain socially involved - Social interaction helps ward off depression and stress, both of which can contribute to memory loss. Look for opportunities to connect with family, friends, and others, especially if you live alone. Solitary confinement can contribute to brain loss.

God has created us to be in fellowship with other people. I believe that is why fellowship is such an important part of our life because it keeps our brain healthy!

"Greater love has no one than this, that a person will lay down his life for his friends."

John 15:13

Most people in North America have heard Jesus is the son of God and Saviour, although some people reject that He is God. However, in the Bible, Jesus confirms that He is God.[3] Jesus was born of a woman to become human, able to "sympathize with our weakness", but conceived as the divine son of God, born to die for our sins.[4] Even though Jesus had the full power of God, He gave up the privileges of Heaven to live in a limited body.[5] After the resurrection, Jesus was still in body form and could be touched, but now He was not limited by the body, so He could just appear to the disciples in a locked house. The proof of Jesus' resurrection was that He appeared to the disciples many times and to over five hundred people within the 40 days before He ascended to Heaven.[6] As we look at other scripture verses, we will find more evidence of why Jesus is worthy of our trust!

First, Jesus was baptized by John not because of sin but to link John's prophecy with His first public act of ministry. Jesus told John to baptize Him so they would be obedient to God's plan to fulfill all

---

[3] John 14:8-10
[4] Matthew 1:18-25, Hebrews 4:14-15 NAS, Matthew 1:21
[5] Philippians 2:6-7
[6] I Corinthians 15:4-8, Acts 1:9

righteousness by completing God's will. When Jesus came out of the water, the Spirit of God descended like a dove on Him, which was God's Spirit, anointing Jesus for success in ministry. Then God's voice came from Heaven, "This is my beloved son, in whom I'm well-pleased," which confirmed God's love for Jesus as a son and that He was pleased with Jesus because of His obedience in baptism to begin His ministry.[7] Jesus' next step was to be led by the Spirit into the wilderness to be tempted by the devil. After Jesus had fasted for 40 days and nights His body was at a point of starvation. The devil waited to appear to Jesus at a weak point. Satan used the same three temptations he uses for everyone by making the *world*, *flesh*, and *his lies* seem appealing. He twisted God's word, but Jesus used the power of the true word of God to defeat him and told him to flee.[8] The time Jesus spent in the wilderness was to recognize His humanity to be able to relate to us. It would also be an example to us of the power we also can use to overcome temptation.[9]

The first disciples Jesus invited to join Him were four fishermen, and He told them in Matthew 4:19, "Follow me, and I will make you fishers of men." This phrase was to relate the importance of their mission to bring people into the kingdom of God as their new way of life. Jesus modeled the method of discipleship as He taught the disciples important principles and got them active in ministry. Jesus's love and patience in working with the disciples is what has made it possible for people to hear about the Good News of Jesus today.[10] Jesus was a great example to us as He shared a close relationship with the Father in prayer and obedience to do nothing of His own initiative but to please the Father.[11] An example of that

---

[7] Matthew 3:13-17 NAS
[8] Matthew 4:1-11
[9] James 4:7
[10] John 15:10-14
[11] Luke 5:16, John 8:28-29

is in Luke 22:42-44 where Jesus was sweating drops of blood because He could foresee the agony it would be as He would be tortured and crucified, but still wanted to do His Father's will. John chapter 19 explains the brutal death Jesus went through at the hands of the Romans so we could have eternal life. Even though Jesus was with the disciples for three years, they did not fully understand the outcome of Jesus' ministry, death, and resurrection. However, after the resurrection, they spent time with Jesus for those 40 days, and then they began to understand more. In Acts 1:3-9 before Jesus ascended into Heaven, He told the disciples to wait for the Holy Spirit before they began their new ministry.

Jesus explained the whole plan of salvation in John 3:2-10 when a Jewish leader named Nicodemus came to ask Jesus questions. Nicodemus was confused because Jesus told Him you must be "born again," then Jesus had to explain further that it was not of the body but being born of the Spirit to enter the kingdom of God. In John 14:1- 6, it says that there is no other name except Jesus Christ that can save us from our sins. Some people may think they are good enough because they have never committed any major sins, but Romans 3:23 says everyone has sinned and falls short of what God accepts. This means to be acceptable to God, everyone needs to repent and invite Jesus into their life.[12] After we accept Jesus into our lives, the Holy Spirit comes in to make us new creatures, teach us, guide us, and give us power.[13] Since we can't see Jesus, "we walk by faith, not by sight", then we are no longer under the law, but we live under grace and have direct access to God through prayer because of Jesus' death on the cross.[14]

---

[12] Romans 10:9-10
[13] II Corinthians 5:17, John 16:13, II Timothy 11:7
[14] II Corinthians 5:7 NAS, Romans 6:14, Hebrews 4:16

We can trust Jesus by giving our life to Him because He proved His love for us when He died on the cross to give us eternal life.

As Christians after all Jesus has done and continues to do in our life, He is worthy of our trust!

PROTECTING OUR HEART HEALTH

The heart is a symbol of love and compassion, but we know our emotions come from an area of our brain. Since the brain controls the body's nervous system, that means it controls the heart too. Both our brain and emotions have an important role in our love and trust of Jesus. As Christians, we talk about accepting Jesus into our hearts, knowing that it is His Holy Spirit that comes to live within us as our helper to live the Christian life. Our heart is our life-giving source that is impossible to live without, just as Jesus is our life-giving source to live in the Spirit. So, we are going to look at the functions of the heart and how we can protect our heart to keep it strong.

Coronary Heart disease is the leading cause of death for men, women, and people of most racial and ethnic groups. Heart disease is a catch-all phrase for a variety of conditions that affect the heart's structure and function. Coronary heart disease is a type of heart disease that develops when the arteries of the heart cannot deliver enough oxygen-rich blood to the heart. This usually caused by the build-up of plaque, a waxy substance, inside the lining of the larger coronary arteries. This build-up can partially or totally block blood flow in the large arteries of the heart. Sometimes this condition may be caused by disease or injury affecting how the arteries work in the heart. Coronary microvascular disease is another type of coronary heart disease. It occurs when the heart's tiny blood vessels do not work normally.

We are led to believe that we need to watch our cholesterol to prevent a heart attack. Yet studies have shown that in 75% of heart attack patients, cholesterol levels were normal. Most of the cholesterol circulating in the body is made within the body, not from the food you eat. Cholesterol is a substance made in the liver that is vital to human life. In the body, cholesterol serves three main purposes: it aids in the production of sex hormones, is a building block for human tissue, and assists in bile production in the liver. It is the oxidized form of cholesterol that is a significant component of the substance that makes up arterial plaque. Reducing the amount of cholesterol circulating in your blood has no relation to the oxidation of cholesterol or to the laying down of plaque in the arteries. The main culprits for heart attacks are sugars, which are a result of refined carbohydrates and trans fats. Plaque occurs because of injury to the artery wall, which happens because sugars stick to the protein fibers that make up the artery, and it is injured by oxidation. The sugars from the trans fats contribute to inflammation, which is responsible for the continued laying down of plaque.

Trans fats are manufactured oils called hydrogenated oils. In the body they become sugars that cause the arteries to become sticky, which makes it harmful to our heart. Most trans fats are found in margarine, commercially fried foods, bakery products made with shortening, margarine, or hydrogenated oils. Products include crackers, cookies, donuts, cakes, pastries, muffins, croissants, snack foods, fried foods such as French fries and breaded foods. It is best to avoid these foods unless you want to make your own with healthy ingredients. For your heart, it is best to avoid, or limit refined sugar, hydrogenated oils, refined flour, processed food, fried foods, candy, alcohol, acidic fruits, and anything that causes inflammation in the body.

The body has the amazing ability to heal itself when you stay away from things that can be harmful to your health and give it the nutrients it needs to repair and strengthen. The natural supplements that help in the repair of the heart are Collagen, Vitamin C, and Lysine (amino acid). Other supplements that keep the heart strong include fish Oil (omega 3s), which helps keep inflammation down; Garlic helps thin blood and keeps blood pressure down; Hawthorn strengthens the heart contractions; Lecithin helps to break down bad fats, and Niacin (B 3) helps to keep arteries clear. Magnesium is an important nutrient for the heart, helping to regulate blood pressure, helps with irregular heartbeat, block arteries, and regulates blood pressure. When a person is taken to the hospital with a heart attack, the doctors give them an injection with magnesium to relax the heart.

A TEMPLE FOR THE HOLLY SPIRIT

"Do you not know you are a temple of God, and that the Spirit of God dwells in you?"

I Corinthians 3:16

Do we fully understand the Holy Spirit? Most Christians know that the Holy Spirit is the third person of the Trinity, but it is important to realize He is not less in power. He has the same power that worked in creation; the same power that enabled the great men of God in the Old Testament to live their lives for God; the same powder that enabled prophets to speak things that are yet to come; and the same power that was with the Lord Jesus, empowering Him to do miracles and raise from the grave three days after His death. In John 14:26, Jesus begins to tell the disciples His plans to leave and explains the Holy Spirit will be their helper. At that point, the disciples did not totally understand why the Holy Spirit needed to come because they did not understand Jesus would die on the cross and later ascend to Heaven. In Mark 16:19, when Jesus ascended to Heaven, they looked up and saw that Jesus' purpose after His death was to sit at the right hand of His Father in Heaven to rule. When the Holy Spirit came, they realized He came to help them continue the ministry Jesus had started. When we hear the message of salvation and then ask Jesus into our hearts, the Holy Spirit comes to live within us right then as our helper. God, Jesus, and the Holy Spirit have the same characteristics as they work together as one in our life, and they will be with us forever.[15] The Trinity can be a difficult concept to understand because it seems God exists externally as three distinct persons. I Corinthians 12:4-6 talks about varieties of gifts, ministries, and effects, but they are from the same Spirit, Lord, and God. It helps me to think of each one as having a unique role in our lives. God our creator, who we go to directly in prayer because of Jesus; Jesus the son that came as God in the flesh to relate to humans and made a way to God; and the Holy Spirit came to take the place of Jesus, then He could live within us to help live a righteous life for God and to tell others of Jesus. My husband uses the example of water which can become steam and turn to ice, but all 3 three are water.

An important aspect of the Holy Spirit is our personal relationship with Him. In Ephesians 1:13 it tells us that when we ask Jesus into our life, we become "sealed in Him with the Holy Spirit of promise," and that makes the Holy Spirit an intricate part of our lives. We then have the Holy Spirit inside of us to guide and teach us; our part is to be sensitive to His leading. To accomplish that, we need to keep a close relationship with God through prayer, reading the Bible, and allowing the Holy Spirit to work through us in our giftings. In I Thessalonians, we are told not to quench (extinguish) the power of the Holy Spirit, and then Paul tells us a few things we can do to avoid that.[16] Then, in Ephesians, Paul tells us how important it is to "lay aside our old self" and gives us further instructions on how we should act since we are filled with the Spirit.[17] In Ephesians 4:30, he tells us not to grieve (make sad) the Holy Spirit and list some things we should eliminate and replace them with kindness and

---

[15] 1 John 5:4-7, John 14:16-17
[16] I Thessalonians 5:19-22 NAS
[17] Ephesians 4:22-29 NAS

forgiveness.[18] When we choose to sin, we are being disobedient not only to God's commands but the leadings of the Holy Spirit to do what is right.

Paul says, "Your body is the temple (home) of the Holy Spirit who is in you, whom you have from God, and you are not your own" because you have been bought by the precious blood of Jesus. "Therefore, glorify God in your body."[19] Since our body is the temple of the Holy Spirit, how should we treat our body? When we think of a temple, we think of it as a holy place to worship God. The Hebrew meaning of Holy is set apart for a purpose. In 1 Corinthians 6:18, the verse talks about fleeing from sexual sin because "every other sin that man commits is outside the body," but sexual sin is against our body, which is the temple of the Holy Spirit. The illustration that Paul used is when a man joins himself to a woman, "the two become one flesh," and when you join yourself, "to the Lord you are one spirit with Him."[20] Sexual sin not only grieves the Holy Spirit, but it breaks that Holy bond that we have with God. However, God is always loving and forgiving when we come to Him and repent, as it tells us in I John 1:9, and that is the only way to rebuild that spiritual bond again. When you commit sexual sin, you also cause consequences in your life because of deep hurt to family and friends. Once those relationships become damaged, it is not always easy to rebuild them again.

To take care of our temple it involves taking care of our physical body. In Genesis 1:29, God instructed Adam and Eve that every seed-bearing plant and fruit tree was their food. Later in Genesis 9:2-4, God told Noah that every fish from the sea, every moving

---

[18] Ephesians 4:30-32
[19] 1 Corinthians 6:19-20 NAS
[20] 1 Corinthians 6:16-17 NAS

thing that is alive, is for their food, plus the plants that already were given to them for food. However, they were not to eat the flesh with the blood. In North America, we live in a fast-paced society, so eating healthy is not that simple and that contributes to many people consuming more fast food. Even our food in the grocery stores are over-processed which make vegetables and meat unnatural. Unless the food meets organic standards, our food lacks nutrition. Paul reminds us in I Corinthians 10:31, "Whether then, you eat or drink or whatever you do, do all to the Glory of God."

Then, if we do everything to glorify God, we will take care of our temple by making good choices as we eat. This will give us a better quality of life, and then we can live a fruitful life to minister more effectively for God.

KEEPING OUR TEMPLE HEALTHY

We learned in our spiritual life we need to maintain a pure condition in our temple, for the Holy Spirit. Since our body is the temple of the Holy Spirit, we should try to maintain the health of our body, too. That will give us a better quality of life to serve the Lord as the Holy Spirit leads and guides us.

Our body was perfect when God created it. However, sin came into the world and not only put a division between God and humans, but it began the decay of our bodies, sickness, and disease. God has given us amazing bodies to care for, and if we give our bodies the nutrients it needs, that can prevent or heal disease. I have found that many people think their body can take care of itself if they try to eat the best they can. That is like saying we do not need to go to church because we can just read our Bible at home to be strong in our Christian faith. However, the Bible tells us that we need the fellowship of others too. Just like our bodies will let us know, we need something more than just food when our health starts to break down. That is because we need preventative measures to take care of our bodies. We live in an environment that can be toxic, so we need to give our bodies the defense it needs to stay healthy.

Sickness and disease seem to come into our lives at some point for ourselves, family, and friends. Knowing the cause of illness and disease will help us understand how to prevent and/or correct it. A good example of something occurring in the body that causes disease and illness is catarrh. This is mucous produced as a consequence of tissue inflammation. Catarrh is developed when the eliminative organs, which are the kidneys, skin (largest organ), bowel, bronchial plus lung structure, and the lymph system are not working efficiently. If elimination is obstructed in the body, the catarrh may be forced to settle in the weaker organs and tissue. This causes issues for various organs to get inflamed, like the appendix, called appendicitis; the bronchi is bronchitis; the joints are arthritis, and the nose is rhinitis, to name. So, as you see anything caused by inflammation, the spelling of the description has *itis* at the end. When a person has unhealthy eating habits that continue regularly, it can eventually affect the whole body because it causes inflammation. Examples of the cause would be consuming an excess of products with refined sugars, refined flour, candy, pop, juices, acidic fruit, tap water, meat, coffee, and even stress. These things put a burden on the digestive system because they kill off beneficial bacteria in the intestines. It also causes an imbalance in the pH levels, which makes us prone to colds, depletes the minerals from the body, which affect our teeth, and bones, which are only a few of the effects.

Everything in life has a cause and effect because things do not just happen on their own, and our health is the same. Prevention is always the best medicine when it comes to our health. We can help to avoid sickness and disease if we take precautions to eat well by eating organic food when we can and especially try to avoid fast foods that are bad for our health. We need 80% of our food to be alkaline and know that all protein is acidic. There are acid/alkaline food charts that you can search for on Google and print. Then you can put it on the fridge so that will help make it easier to determine the best food choices as you prepare meals. We can try our best to eat well, but most people cannot always eat perfectly. We also live in an ever-changing, toxic world, so we need to get help from supplements to give our bodies a better chance to fight. There are essential supplements to help our body fight off the effects of the environment such as Multivitamins, B 100, buffered Vitamin C, Greens, Probiotics, Fiber, Digestive Enzymes, and Fish Oils.

Hopefully, you will find these health tips helpful, so you can enjoy the benefits of serving God with a healthy temple.

PRINCIPLES OF FAITH

God has given my husband and myself a heart to disciple new Christians. We feel it is important for them to grow in their faith and live the abundant life God wants to give them. Most everything in life has basic principles as the foundation, and our faith in Jesus is no different. Let us discover the basic principles from the Bible that serve as the foundation for our spiritual growth.

Having head knowledge about God, Jesus, and the Holy Spirit is not enough. That is why it is important to remember the time you personally received Jesus into your life because that will give you the assurance that you were born again in the Spirit.[21] To receive Jesus into your life, you go to God in true sorrow for not living a life pleasing to Him (repent) and acknowledge (confess) that you need Jesus to come into your life to make you the kind of person He wants you to be.[22] That is when you received *Salvation* because God forgave your sins when you accepted that Jesus's death was for you. There was nothing you could do to earn your way to Heaven, so now you are living by grace and have eternal life.[23] God does not take us to Heaven right away because He wants us to tell others about Jesus.[24]

Baptism is the first step after salvation, which symbolizes your death from sin and being raised to living right before God. [25] When you are baptized, it is the first step to being obedient to God. You can show an outward expression of the inward change that has taken place in your life after you accept Jesus. In the New

---

[21] John 3:3
[22] Romans 10:9-11
[23] John 3:16, Ephesians 2:8-9
[24] I Peter 3:15
[25] Romans 6:3-11

Testament, they would do baptism immediately after acceptance of Jesus, but now it is not practical. So, it is important to find a good Bible-believing *church* to attend as soon as possible and then you can be baptized there. Attending a church helps you learn more about God's word so you can grow in your faith. Also, you will be with other like-minded people who can encourage you in your spiritual walk.[26] In the New Testament, they did not have buildings for churches, but people committed to meeting in homes. Now, we attend church in a building to be committed to each other and its ministries. We are now born-again Christians who are considered a part of the Body of Christ, which the Bible also refers to as the church.[27] You can be further committed to a local church by becoming a *Member.* This is like committing to becoming a part of the family of God. While attending church, you build a bond with others as you worship together and serve God through the church ministries. *Tithing* is an important responsibility since God has given us everything. Whether we have much or little, we give according to what God puts in our hearts to give. It is important as a member of a church to support it financially as a way to show commitment to the church. In Leviticus 27:30, it says that they were required to give 10% of their crops to God (temple) and that anything extra was an offering. Most often, people in the church today still use the 10% guideline with their money. The New Testament does not list a percentage to give because it says in II Corinthians 9:7 that it is more about each person's heart attitude, by giving what they can cheerfully. *Communion* is an important part of our faith that Jesus commanded us to do as a remembrance of what He has done for us.[28] Originally, Jesus and the disciples had

---

[26] Hebrews 10:24- 25
[27] I Corinthians 12:27, Colossians 1:18
[28] Luke 22:14-20

real bread and wine to symbolize His body and blood, which He would give to save us. However, it is not practical to do that in church now, so most churches use crackers and grape juice for communion once a month. The important thing is not what kind of bread we eat, whether we use wine, or how often we have communion but to be obedient to Jesus' command to observe the remembrance of His life for ours. As we remember Christ's death on the cross it renews our awareness of His love for us and rekindles our love and commitment to Him.

Our commitment to God should also be outside the church. We need to read the *Bible* daily to provide our daily spiritual food source to live a Spirit-filled life. The Bible teaches us about God's character, promises, keeps us from sin, gives direction, renews our minds, and helps us to know His will.[29] *Prayer is* the privilege of being able to talk directly to God because of what Jesus did on the cross. It is so important to pray every day to keep our communication open to God. [30] *Spiritual Gifts* are given by God to everyone who accepts Jesus into their life.

God gives every believer at least one gift and to some people even more. The number of gifts may increase as you grow spiritually. One of my gifts that God has blessed me with is using my organizational abilities for the gift of administration. Although most spiritual gifts are an ability that does not come naturally but is God given to minister to others inside and outside the church. Paul relates the human body to the Body of Christ since a body has many parts (members) that have different purposes but work together for the body to function properly.[31]

---

[29] Hebrews 6:11-12, Psalm 119:11, Psalm 119:105, Romans 12:2
[30] Hebrews 4:15-16, Philippians 4:6
[31] Romans 12:4-8, I Corinthians 12:4-30

When we follow God's principles, the Bible gives us a special promise that we will not stumble. [32]

---

[32] II Peter 1:4-10

PRINCIPLES FOR HEALTH

Just as there are principles to follow to grow in our faith, there are also principles for good health. So, we are going to look at a few basic principles for the body that can help maintain or improve your health.

Colon Health (large intestine) - In embryology, you learn that the first organ formed in the Ebro is the colon, and every organ blossoms from the colon. That makes it a main reflex point for the health of the body. However, most doctors and people do not realize the importance of having three bowel movements daily for a healthy colon. Regular bowel movements are important to prevent toxic build-up in the body and it can affect how clean the blood will be. Regular bowel movements will prevent bowel-related diseases like diverticulitis, colitis, and Crohn's disease which affect the whole body's health. Another reason the colon is key to good health is that 60% of the immune system resides there. It is also a muscle, so it needs exercise. You can exercise the colon by ensuring you are eating fruits and vegetables for fibre and avoiding a lot of processed food and mushy foods like bagels and white bread. It is good to clean your produce with a fruit & veggie wash to remove parasites, dirt, and chemical residue. The colon helps prevent dehydration of the body, and that makes it important to drink two liters of water each day which will also prevent constipation. Most intestinal flu is waterborne, so it is important to drink purified water. If you are unable to have regular bowel movements, a helpful thing to do first is a colon cleanse. I recommend that everyone should take a fiber supplement and probiotic each day to keep the colon clean and build up healthy bacteria to keep it healthy. After the cleanse, if you are still struggling with constipation, take a natural laxative as long as you need it, but do not take senna or cascara sagrada because the colon will become dependent on it. We should have 80% good bacteria and 20% bad bacteria living in the colon to keep a healthy balance. A majority of people have the good bacteria being depleted because of bad eating habits, medications, and lifestyles. This makes the colon unbalanced, making us more susceptible to parasites because it becomes a friendly environment where they can live. We can acquire parasites from soil, vegetables, fruit, meat, and water. Supplements that are helpful for the colon are Probiotics, Fiber supplement consisting of Ground Flax-Psyllium hull blend, Aloe Vera Juice (keeps pH balance), and, if necessary, a natural laxative just as needed. If you struggle with constipation, Psyllium can cause more constipation if you do not drink enough water, so it is best to get a fiber blend with L-Glutamine, which also can help with any irritable bowel problems.

Diet - Most people find it hard to stay away from junk food. Even when you go to the grocery store, you do not see a lot of good nutritious food. You would think fruits, vegetables, and meat are good for you, but you need to consider how vegetables are grown or how animals are raised. Most soil is overused and nutrient-dense, so artificial nutrients are added, and herbicides and pesticides are used. Most livestock are given genetically modified grains, antibiotics, and growth hormones. Then there is food processing, in which they use preservatives and sometimes color and taste enhancers. The testing done on organically grown spinach proved it had 100% more iron content than regular-grown spinach. In organic farming the soil is not depleted of important nutrients from over-farming and use of chemicals, which makes organic food more nutritious. It is wise to avoid refined sugars, flour, processed foods, red meat, and pop because they cause inflammation in the body, which also depletes the body of calcium. Cane sugar is a better choice than artificial sweeteners because it has a lower glycemic level than refined white sugar and that makes it easier for the body to break down. Artificial sweeteners like Aspartame can cause high blood pressure and other side effects if used continually. Suppose you have diabetes or want a natural sweetener that has zero sugar. In that case, you can use stevia, xylitol, or Erythritol, which are natural plant sugars that do not affect your sugar balance or weight. Read labels, and if you are unsure of all the ingredients, google them to know what you are eating. Also, as you read the labels, you will see fat free is usually hydrogenated oils and sugar-free is Aspartame, which both are harmful to your health. All oils, by nature, go rancid quickly, and the oils at the grocery stores have been altered to prevent them from becoming rancid. It is better to buy unrefined oils that are cold pressed in dark bottles, and refrigerated after they are opened to keep them from going rancid. The oils that do not become carcinogenic when heated are coconut, safflower, and extra virgin olive oil but avoid cooking them on a high temperature.

Exercise - Everyone needs an exercise routine every day. Remaining active helps all the body systems work more efficiently. The best type of exercise is minimal impact, such as biking, walking, or palettes. If you can walk three times a week for 20 minutes, it benefits the cardiovascular system, and has more benefits than just building muscles. The most helpful supplements for Cardiovascular Health are Fish Oil, CoQ10, Garlic, Hawthorne, and Magnesium.

Herbs & Vitamin Supplements - Even if we think we are eating nutritious foods, everyone needs to supplement their diet with multivitamins, since no one can always eat perfectly. As you choose a multivitamin, try to find ones blended with herbs, omega oils, or food base to help the body absorb them better and always take vitamins with a meal. I do not recommend taking high-potency vitamins because it is difficult for the body to absorb large amounts of vitamins in one dose. Most natural vitamins are less potent, so it is suggested to take one capsule with each meal for better absorption. When dealing with areas of weakness in the body, Herbs are beneficial because each herbal plant contains vitamins and minerals. The single Herb or Herb blends give you the nutrients needed for areas that are weak in the body, which will help strengthen and heal. Herbs work best because they go into the body and absorbed like food, which helps the nutrients to be absorbed better. Vitamin C and B Complex are the only water-soluble vitamins that do not build up toxins like fat-soluble vitamins such as A, E, and D. When living in the north, everyone needs extra vitamin D, especially in the winter. Also, vitamin D is especially good for women to take for bone health. It is best to take Vitamin D in emulsified drops under the tongue, so it absorbs better and does not build up toxins. When you take any B vitamins, you need to take them with a B complex to help with absorption. Other required supplements are antioxidants which help prevent cancer, Greens to balance the pH in the body, and extra Proteins for the muscles.

WE ARE ON OUR WAY

"For our citizenship is in heaven, from which also we eagerly wait for a Savior, the Lord Jesus Christ;"

Philippians 3:20

There are quite a few people in the world who are unsure if they will make it to Heaven, and this includes even people who are born-again Christians. Before we look at what Heaven is like, we will focus on God's promises of assurance for eternal life. Hopefully, the promises from God's word will assure you of your eternal security. It will also be exciting to get a glimpse from the Bible what your new home in Heaven will be like.

In Luke 3:15-18 we read that the first person to proclaim that there was eternal life in Jesus was John the Baptist. In John's message, he foretells that Jesus is coming by preaching the gospel and baptizing. Jesus mentions eternal life throughout the gospels, but when a Jewish ruler named Nicodemus asks questions, Jesus gives him a complete definition of what he needs to do to receive eternal life. Nicodemus assumed Jesus was from God because of Jesus knowledge and signs of miracles, but he did not fully understand who Jesus was and His purpose. Jesus told him that he could not go to Heaven unless he was born again, and Nicodemus questioned Jesus further to understand. Jesus explained that you are not being reborn of the flesh again but of the Spirit. Then Jesus goes on to further explain that happens only when you believe in Him to

33

receive eternal life.[33] Jesus also gives us many promises for our salvation in the book of John with statements like, He won't cast us out, no one can snatch us from His hand, we are sealed in Him, which are promises for our eternal security.[34] John explains, as he writes in I John 5:10-13, the confirmation of the promises of eternal security, and then ends his statements that he wrote these things so, "You may <u>know</u> you have eternal life." Although it is good to remember with every promise God gives us in the Bible there is a premise, which means you need to take action to take hold of the promise. This does not mean we are working for our salvation because in Ephesians 2:8-9 it says it is a free gift. The book of James 2:26 says, "For just as the body without the spirit is dead, so also faith without works is dead." Our works are an overflow of our love for God and what Jesus did for us. This makes us want to please Him by keeping the commandments.[35] Jesus said that true Christians will be known by their fruit and love for one another.[36] When we take hold of God's promise of eternal life, how can we not feel secure in knowing we are going to Heaven?

A few years back, when my children were younger, there was a song we liked to sing in church about Heaven. The chorus was, "Heaven is a wonderful place, filled with glory and grace. I want to see my Savior's face cause Heaven is a wonderful palace. I want to go there!" Jesus tells us in John 14:2- 6 that there are many dwelling places in His Father's house and that He will prepare a place for us so we can be with Him. We are told we will have new bodies that won't get sick, no need for marriage as we have here on earth, and no more tears, death, or pain.[37] There will be no need for temples

---

[33] John 3:1-16
[34] John 5:24, 6:37-40, 10:27-29 NAS
[35] John 14:15,21
[36] Matthew 7:15-20, John 13:34-35
[37] Philippians 3:20-21, Matthew 22:30, Revelation 21:4

because God and Jesus are our temple, and no day or night because God is our continual light.[38] Heaven is a beautiful place that defies description and understanding of how it looks exactly. In Revelations, it says God is sitting on the throne and describes it as a jasper stone and a ruby in appearance, plus there was a rainbow around the throne like an emerald in appearance. Also from the throne were flashes of lightning plus sounds of thunder with a sea of glass-like crystal, and in the center around the throne angels were praising the Lord.[39] Heaven is described more when it comes down to earth after the tribulation. It has a great high wall which was like jasper, and the city streets are pure gold, like clear glass. The foundation stones of the city were adorned with every kind of precious stone, and the twelve gates each contained a single pearl.[40] It all sounds so beautiful, and according to commentaries, each item represents something about Heaven. Revelation 21:8 clearly explains who will not be in Heaven and as bad as the people seem that are on this list, God loves all His children. He would have let them into Heaven if they had only accepted Jesus while on earth when they had a chance and left their evil life behind. Our goal should be to tell more people about Jesus so everyone will get a chance to make a choice where they will spend eternity. It tells us in II Peter 3:9 that God is patient with us because He does not want anyone to perish but to come to repentance. In Revelations 21:27, it states the only ones allowed into heaven will have their name in the *Lamb's* (Jesus) *Book of Life*.

---

[38] Revelation 21:22-27
[39] Revelation 4:3-11
[40] Revelation 21:12-21

I am sure Heaven will be beautiful because the glory of God will be all around us. When we see Jesus, we will bow down to worship Him, and any questions we have now will all be forgotten.

We may not completely know what to expect of Heaven, but it tells us of Jesus in I John 3:2 "We know when He appears, we shall be like Him, because we will see Him just as He is."

BENEFITS OF RELAXATION

Nothing can compare with Heaven! We can rest in the assurance that God promises eternal life, and no one can take that away from us. However, in our everyday lives, finding time to relax can be difficult. We are going to look at the health benefits of relaxation and the things we can do to relax.

Daily stress can take a toll not only on physical but our mental health. Stress also puts us at risk of heart disease and high blood pressure. Everyone has days that are busy, but most people have a stressful lifestyle, and those who overwork themselves suffer from burnout. So, it has become more important to make time to relax. Did you know there are scientifically proven health benefits of travel? Studies have found you need at least eight days away for it to be beneficial. When we travel, it makes us happy to be in new locations and see new sights. It is easier for me to forget the stress and relax just by being away in another location. It not only puts us in a happy mindset that relieves stress but may also promote more physical activity that we may not be getting at our job or at home. When it comes to vacations, a lot of people do not have the extra money to travel. However, there are always other travel options that are not as costly as flying.

You can get away to various locations by going camping in your tent or trailer. Road trips can be fun to stay at hotels or Bed & Breakfast as you travel or drive to a destination hotel. On one of our anniversaries, my husband planned a trip to New York City for a live theatre production and a stay at a hotel in Times Square. We live north of Toronto, Ontario, so we decided to make it a road trip there. We stayed on the way there and back at beautiful historical

Bed and Breakfast homes. When we arrived in New York City we went on a bus tour around the city to see the sights and learn the history of distinct locations. It was a trip we will never forget! My husband and I have a larger boat we purchased a few years ago. So, we take a weeks' vacation in the summer through the waterways and also enjoy going away to a port for a couple of weekends too. Then, on weekends, we ask friends or family to go out with us on the boat for a day or evening cruise.

Studies show that various forms of relaxation can help reduce many chronic health concerns, restore energy, and encourage a more positive sense of self. When we cannot always get away, there are things you can do right at home to help you relax. You can do simple things like walks, biking, crafts, naps, or reading, which all promote health benefits. Just doing simple things can ease anxiety and depression, boost your energy, think more clearly, and handle stress better. You can even go for a massage to relax your muscles. It is good for everyone to set aside time for themselves and spend time with their family.

There are also supplements that can help you relax while having a busy lifestyle. Of course, we need our sleep to function, but many people just have trouble sleeping, so melatonin can help. Supplements that are helpful for the body to relax and manage stress better are B-100, Natural Factors-Mental Calm chewable, Rescue Remedy, and powdered magnesium. Place the magnesium in hot water and make a nice relaxing drink for bedtime.

THE GREATEST GIFT EVER

"Every good thing bestowed and every perfect gift is from above,"

James 1:17

Most people enjoy getting gifts! Usually, giving a gift can be special for the giver and the receiver. However, sometimes, the giver does not think out what the receiver really needs or wants. If it is something they do not want they will set it aside and regift it. Even if we do not understand the purpose of a gift, we will never be disappointed with God's gifts because they are always good and perfect. We are going to look in the Bible at the gifts from God.

God is our creator, so He does not have to guess or ask us what we want since He knows our needs intimately. In the first two chapters of Genesis, He gave us the gift of *life* and *provisions* for life. God did not make us like robots because He wanted a relationship with us, so He gave us the gift of *free will* to make our own choices.[41] The gift of the *law* of the *commandments* were given to teach us right and wrong for our *protection.* In Galatians 3:24, Paul explains how the law is also our tutor that leads us to Christ. This leads us to the *most important gift* we needed because of our sin, which was our gift of *salvation* through Jesus' death on the cross.[42] When we become Christians, we are saved by God's gift of *grace,* and now we live under *grace* instead of the law.[43] When we accept Jesus, we receive the gift of the *Holy Spirit* as our helper.[44] In Ephesians 1:4 it tells us

---

[41] Deuteronomy 30:19
[42] Romans 6:23
[43] Ephesians 2:8, Romans 6:14
[44] Acts 2:38, John 14:26

we are now seen as *holy* and *blameless* before God, which is a gift. We can go directly to God through the gift of *prayer* since Jesus is our high priest.[45] As God's children, we experience the gift of His *love* and *discipline* as a parent. We have the gift of His *loving-kindness, mercy, and faithfulness, which are new every* day.[46] In John 10:10, Jesus says He has come to give us an *abundant life*. I came from a very dysfunctional family, but in my new abundant life, God is my Father, plus He has blessed me with a wonderful family, home, and Christian friends. God has given Christians so many gifts that it would be difficult to list them all.

In God's gifts for ministry, He gives each individual Christian at least one *gift to equip* them for service. In Romans 12:6 it says that God has given us gifts that differ according to the grace given to each Christian. The gifts are listed in three different epistles in the Bible that include in the list; apostles, prophets, evangelists, pastors, teachers, exhortation, knowledge, wisdom, helps, hospitality, giving, administration, mercy, faith, discernment, leaders, healing, miracles, and various tongues, which all are given by the same Spirit.[47] Jesus appointed the first *Apostles*. Today this gift has similar goals as in the past, such as the ability to minister cross-culturally and plant churches. *Prophecy* is the ability to use the authoritative word of God's truth to reveal God's will and helps us understand things to come. *Evangelism* is the ability to be a productive instrument of God in bringing souls to Jesus. *Pastors* have the special ability to effectively feed, guide, and protect a flock of followers in Christ. *Teaching* is a special ability to give a detailed understanding of Biblical truths. *Exhortation* is to come alongside another Christian to encourage, challenge, or advise. *Knowledge* is

---

[45] Hebrews 4:14-16
[46] Lamentations 3:22-23
[47] Romans 12:5-8, I Corinthians 12:4-11,28, Ephesians 4:11

the ability to master God's truths in scripture and discern truth from falsehood. *Wisdom* is an intimate understanding of God's word and his commandments which result in living right before God. *Helps is* the ability to provide timely assistance. *Hospitality* is the ability to provide food, lodging, fellowship, and the ability to welcome people to make them feel loved. *Giving* is the ability to show your faith by giving generously to the Lord's work. *Administration* is the ability to work with followers of God toward organizational objectives for ministry. *Mercy* is the ability to show compassion to those who are struggling with something or suffering. *Faith* is the unusual ability to trust the power of God and act on it. *Discernment* is the ability to distinguish truth from false and good from evil. *Leadership* is the ability to set goals, motivate, and lead others toward an accomplishment. There are also supernatural gifts such as *healing*, *miracles*, and *tongues* that can only be performed through God's supernatural powers. Sometimes, as Christians, we do not understand what our spiritual gifts are. First, it is good to know that gifts are given to us through God's grace and not by our goodness or worthiness. It tells us in Romans 12:6-8 to exercise our gifts as given to us by grace. If you are uncertain of your gifts, and your church does not have a questionnaire, you can Google Spiritual Gift Assessment Questionnaire to help. Our spiritual gifts are given to help us minister to others, and God intends for us to use them as the Spirit leads. God gives gifts that are based on His character of being good, not on our performance. God's gifts are perfect forever, so they never lose their value.

The *greatest gift* ever given to us was **salvation** through Jesus, who made all other gifts possible.

What will you do with these priceless gifts that God has given you?

THE GIFT OF MENTAL HEALTH

God has also given us such a wonderful gift by giving us our minds to think and experience His love. God has created us uniquely, like the brain, which makes it is difficult to explain. Paul mentions spirit, soul, and body in I Thessalonians 5:23, when his hope is that they may be found blameless when Jesus comes again. The spirit is the part of us that connects or refuses to connect with God. The soul is our intellect and emotions, and that is who we are. Our body is physical, and everything inside was created to make it function. In the temporal lobe of the brain there is a small almond shaped part of the brain called the Amygdala. It is a paired structure in which the two are considered one brain area, but each is in a different hemisphere of the brain, and it is a different color than the brain. It is a major processing center for emotions. It also links your emotions to many other brain abilities, especially memories, learning and your senses. This makes me wonder if this is where the spirit and soul connect. In the process of writing this, I read various articles on the difference between the brain and the mind. It seems there are various opinions among scientists and the neurologist's view. God is so amazing in how he made our brain so intricate, just as the rest of our body, and it baffles the brains or minds of the scientists!

When we think of the mind, we think of Mental Health. Mental illness indirectly affects all Canadians at some time through a family member, friend, or colleague. Mental illness affects people of all ages, education, income levels, and cultures. They say by the age of 40, about 50% of the population will have or have had a mental illness. Suicide is one of the leading causes of death in both men and women. There is a wide range of mental disorders, such as anxiety, depression, schizophrenia, dementia, eating disorders, panic attacks, bipolar and the list goes on. It seems in this lifetime, there are many more people suffering from anxiety and depression who are on medications. The causes can be genetic, biological, personality, and environmental factors. These could all play a role in Mental Health, although it is my belief that we live in a broken world that has a major impact on the cause of mental health.

I will stick to some basic suggestions when recommending natural alternatives for mental health since there is such a wide range of Mental Health issues. The suggestions which are recommended for brain health would also apply to mental health. The key points for mental health are exercise, plenty of sleep, a healthy diet, staying mentally active, and social involvement. Also helpful for mental health is going outside to get away from electronics and distractions to help clear your mind. Plus, talking to a friend or therapist about the things that are bothering you can be helpful.

There are times when mental disorders can be a lack of nutrients for the brain. That is why eating healthy and taking supplements can be helpful. The supplements that are important for mental health are fish oils high in DHA (good fats for the brain), B-100, Vitamin D, L-Theanine (also in Mental Calm chewable), GABA, L- Tyrosine, Gingko Biloba (circulation to the brain), Magnesium (powdered form for absorption, helps to relax the mind), Ashwagandha, (supports the adrenals for stress & anxiety), Valerian, Melatonin (for sleep) and a Probiotic. You should take some precautions before taking some natural supplements if you are on medications. Also, don't rule out the possibility that you may have a high concentration of heavy metals in the body, which can affect the brain, and you can get tested for that through a chelation clinic.

God is full of love for His people and does not enjoy seeing them suffering with mental health. If you do not know Jesus and are struggling with mental health, the acceptance of Jesus into your life will allow you to experience His love and peace during the healing process. It tells us in II Corinthians 1:3-4 that God is the "Father of all mercies and the God of all comfort."

NO ONE IS GOOD

"Jesus said to him, "Why do you call me good? No one is good except God alone."

Mark 10:18

What do you think of when you hear the word good? The Oxford Dictionary says it means that it is morally right; benefit or advantage to someone or something. Most people think they are good because they have not done any really bad things and that everyone has some good in them. There are many scripture references to God being good, and the only reason that people have any good in them at all is because they were created in God's image, but the reality of life on earth is that our sinful nature interferes with us being considered good.[48] We will look at different aspects of God's goodness in the Bible.

In the beginning, God was very pleased with His creation and said it was good. The only thing God felt was not good was that man was alone, so he made that good by creating woman.[49] The pure relationship with God was damaged by Satan's lie and Adam's rebellion, which brought sin into the world. There are many scriptures in the Old Testament where the concept of good focuses on concrete experiences of God actively being good to His people. Two important times in history for the Jewish people were recognized first by Jethro as he declares the goodness of God in the saving act to liberate them from Egypt. Also, Ezra recognizes God's

---

[48] Psalm 145:9, Romans 3:10-12
[49] Genesis 1:31, Genesis 2:18-23

goodness when he is able to come back to Jerusalem with a remnant of His people from captivity in Babylon.[50] Other examples of God being good are through His laws and commandments; His promises; His gifts; and that He works all things for good.[51] Even now, with God's saving Grace, Christians have been saved not because they are good but in order to do good. God promises that He will complete the good work in us that He started.[52]

I find it interesting that when a disaster happens, people question how a good God can allow these things to happen. Most of these people have little or no relationship with God and only recognize Him when they want to blame Him for the bad things that happen. If people truly knew God, they would realize only goodness is a part of His nature. Holiness and righteousness are part of God's nature as well, so He cannot do anything that is unholy or unrighteous. God is Holy, so He does not tempt people to do bad things and finds no pleasure in wickedness.[53] The fact that God is good means that He has no evil in Him, and His intentions and motivations are always good. He always does what is right, and the outcomes of His plans are always good.[54] However, sometimes, it is difficult to understand why God allows certain things to happen in our lives. Although, it can help us better understand if we consider that God can see the beginning to the end of our life, His thoughts are beyond our understanding.[55]

There are examples of situations in the Bible that might make people wonder if God is good. Even though God is good, He is also

---

[50] Exodus 18:9, Ezra 7:6, 27-28
[51] Psalm: 19:7-8, Psalm 84:11, James 1:17, Romans 8:28
[52] Romans 3:23, Ephesians 2:10, Philippians 1:6
[53] James 1:13, Psalm 5:4
[54] Jeremiah 29:11
[55] Isaiah 55:8-9

righteous and just, which makes Him angry with people's ungodliness and unrighteousness. We can look at things that seem unfair, like why did God harden Pharaoh's heart, why did Judas have to take the fall to betray Jesus? God knew that Pharaoh already had a hard heart, but He was giving him a chance to see His power. However, since Pharaoh was not going to change his mind, God gave him over to his hard heart. God did not choose Judas to betray Jesus, but that was an evil motive that came from his heart. It would go against God's nature to be cruel by hardening hearts or causing betrayal. Why were the Jewish people the chosen ones? There were various gods to worship, but Abraham believed in one true God.[56] Since God made a promise to Abraham, He gave his people first choice to accept Jesus as their Messiah. When they rejected the message, He gave the Gentiles a chance for repentance.[57] God loves all His children, so He would not choose only the people He wants. God will give everyone a chance even the people that He knows their hearts will not change.

So why is there so much disaster and evil in the world? God gave Adam rule of the earth, and Adam gave Satan that authority when he allowed Satan to deceive him.[58] Satan deceived Eve by twisting the truth to make it sound right, just like he does with people to this day. God created man and woman to have free will to make their own decisions. Then, because of Satan's deception, they choose to sin against God instead of trusting and obeying what God told them. At that point, everything changed because sin entered the world, and Satan's mission is to cause disaster and evil in the world.[59] God was good when He sent Jesus to give His life for us. God wants no

---

[56] Deuteronomy 7:6-9
[57] Acts 13:46
[58] Genesis 1:26, Genesis 3:1-6
[59] John 10:10

one to perish but everyone to repent and accept Jesus in their life. His ultimate goal for those who accept Jesus is that we can spend eternity with Him in heaven and complete His promise to make everything right.[60] We will always have things in the world and our lives that do not seem good because of the effects of sin. As Christians, we have a good God that will be with us to lead and guide us through life. In Romans 8:28 it is not talking about everything working out good for what we want but to accomplish God's purpose. Then what is God's purpose? It is that everything that has happened in our life can be used to conform us to the image of Christ.[61]

We can trust that our good God knows the purpose of difficulties that come into our lives and how it will benefit us on our journey to heaven as we are being perfected.

---

[60] Revelations 21:4
[61] Romans 8:29

GOOD BENEFITS FROM CINNAMON

God is good, and there is no one else that is good, so it is impossible to compare. However, God has given us a lot of good things to enjoy. One is the spice cinnamon, which most people love because it tastes and smells *good*. One of the exceptions would be my 7-year-old granddaughter, who thinks it is too spicy. Besides cooking with it and enjoying the smell and taste of cinnamon, there are so many other benefits that are *good* for our health. We are going to look at the health benefits and ways to use cinnamon.

Cinnamon is loaded with powerful *antioxidants* that slow the aging process, strengthen the immune system, and protect the body from pathogens like viruses, bacteria, and other harmful free radicals in the environment. Cinnamon is so high in antioxidants that it outranks other powerful antioxidant-rich foods like fruits and vegetables. This amazing spice is particularly rich in polyphenols, a specific type of antioxidant known to help prevent chronic disease.

People have been using cinnamon for thousands of years for both its flavor and medicinal properties. Today, people use it to alleviate tummy troubles and *gastrointestinal discomfort*. In traditional Ayurvedic medicine, cinnamon is commonly used to treat gas and digestive imbalances. A spoonful of honey mixed with cinnamon or a bit of it in your tea is said to relieve indigestion, and cinnamon was also found to soothe gastric ulcers. Though more research is needed to determine how effective it is in soothing the digestive system.

Inflammation is essential to the body's healing process. While short-term inflammation is helpful in fighting infections and healing injuries, research shows that *long-term inflammation* can

51

lead to chronic health conditions. Cinnamon's antioxidants have potent anti-inflammatory properties that can help reduce inflammation in the body. Research shows that cinnamon may be effective for treating and preventing inflammatory conditions. Cinnamon is proven to reduce muscle soreness and may also reduce other types of pain, particularly exercise-related pain. You can purchase the essential oil of cinnamon at your local health food store. It can be applied to sore areas of the body also with a carrier oil like castor oil to massage it into the skin.

Cinnamon may help keep your heart healthy and reduce the risk of *heart disease*. This powerhouse spice lowers cholesterol and blood pressure as well as triglyceride levels in the body, which are all common risk factors for developing heart disease. It also increases and improves circulation. If you have had a heart attack or stroke, cinnamon may help repair damaged heart tissues. Cinnamon can also be purchased in capsule form at your local health food store.

Cinnamon is proclaimed as one of the best spices for *diabetics* because of its ability to lower blood sugar levels. It improves sensitivity to insulin, a hormone that helps transport sugar through the bloodstream to tissues to keep blood sugar levels balanced. Along with eating a healthy, balanced diet for managing diabetes, cinnamon can be helpful in stabilizing blood sugar levels. It even has anti-diabetic effects, as it can significantly lower fasting blood sugar level. You can get cinnamon in bulk and take ½ -1tsp of it in food, honey, or tea once a day. Avoid breathing the powder because it can irritate the lungs.

Usually, people think of fish oil for the brain, but cinnamon may boost brain function and help defend against common age-related *neurological disorders*, such as Alzheimer's disease, because it helps block the build-up of protein in the brain. This means cinnamon may be helpful in preventing cognitive decline as you get older. The antioxidant properties in cinnamon may also protect against oxidative stress, reducing the risk of damage to neurons (brain cells), helping preserve brain function, and keeping your brain sharp and functioning as it should.

There are even toothpastes that contain cinnamon as an ingredient for its *antibacterial* properties, plus it has been used for centuries to help soothe toothaches and fight against mouth disease. It protects against certain bacteria that cause cavities, bad breath, and mouth infections.

It has various benefits for the skin because of *antimicrobial* and *antibiotic* properties that protect the skin from rashes, infections, and irritation. You can apply cinnamon essential oil mixed with almond oil to reduce wrinkles, plus it promotes skin cell growth, and reduces acne and rosacea.

Cinnamon is so surprisingly good smelling and tasting, but even extra good because of all the health benefits too!

THE TRUTH OF THE WORD

"Sanctify them in the truth; Thy word is truth."

John: 17:17

My compassion is teaching God's word to others so they can grow in their understanding of His word. Also, the ultimate goal would be that they know God better and grow in their faith. I Googled statistics on how many church goers read the Bible in Canada; it was shocking: only 11%. The Gallup poll has asked questions about personal views of the Bible in the U.S. every year up to 2022. The people that think the Bible is the literal word of God is now only 20%, which is the lowest it has ever been. Gallup also stated that the Bible has been the bestselling book throughout the years. All the polls may not be completely accurate, but it still is shocking that it would even be close to such low numbers. As a Christian, you hope all the believers in the body of Christ will read their Bible every day. As we read the Bible, we are not depending on our understanding. The Holy Spirit reveals what God wants us to learn from the word, then we can apply it to our life. Let's venture through the Bible to study the truth of God's word.

The Bible as we know it was compiled in 400 A.D. There are 66 books in the Bible that were written over a span of some 1,600 years by 40 men. The greatest historical find was in 1947 when shepherds stumbled upon a cave in a rugged area by the Dead Sea and found scrolls. It was encouraging to read that almost every Old Testament book was discovered, and there were minimal differences when compared to the Hebrew texts produced a thousand years later, which we use today. God's words are so powerful that He spoke creation into existence.[62] God spoke His word to give us the laws to live by for our protection.[63] He spoke words to the prophets to give the people direction, discipline and to foretell the future. He also inspired the disciples to write books about Him and letters to the churches with instructions for living the Christian life. The Bible flows together from Genesis through Revelation, mentioning Jesus throughout both books. That is why it is important to read the Old Testament to understand the history, the problems, the needs of the people, and their relationship with God. The New Testament also refers to people and events in the Old Testament. The Bible would have been abandoned centuries ago if the contents proved to be untrue or ineffective in helping people with their lives. In Isaiah 55:11, God says, "My word shall not return to Me empty, without accomplishing what I desire."

We usually only think of the Bible as the word of God, but the word existed long before the Bible was written. John 1:1 starts with this statement: "In the beginning was the Word, and the Word was with God, and the Word was God." Even the book of Revelation 19:13 refers to Jesus as the "The Word of God." In essence, Jesus is the Word that became flesh, which came to us "full of grace and truth."[64] Jesus said, "I am the way, the truth, and the life," and the Holy Spirit is the Spirit of Truth.[65] Moses said, "God is not a man that He should lie," so when God says something, He means it and will do it.[66] We understand that God is absolute truth, so He can not lie because He never changes.[67] Now that we have established God

---

[62] Genesis 1:1-31
[63] Exodus chapter 20
[64] John 1:14 NAS
[65] John 14:6a, John 16:13 NAS
[66] Numbers 23:19 NAS
[67] Hebrews 6:17-18

is truth, there is nowhere in the Bible that His word is not true since "all scripture is inspired by God" for man to write.[68] When we become believers, the Holy Spirit helps us understand the Bible. However, there will be some things we might not fully comprehend, but that does not mean they aren't the truth.[69]

In Ecclesiastes 3:11, Solomon said God has "set eternity in the human heart". Every human soul has a God-given awareness that there is something more than this momentary world. With that awareness of eternity comes a hope that we can one day find a fulfillment that the world cannot give us. The human heart has not changed over the ages, and neither have the words of God.[70] Only God's word can get through to a man's heart because it is "able to judge the thoughts and intentions of the heart."[71] Romans 10:17 says, "Faith comes by hearing, and hearing by the Word of God." When people receive Jesus as Savior and Lord it changes their lives, gives purpose, peace of mind, and a future for eternity.[72] Through sound Bible teaching, people are introduced to Jesus Christ and grow in their faith through the word.[73]

The Bible is truly the Word of God, so it is the final authority for all matters of faith, and morality. Since the Bible is God's Word, dismissing it would be to dismiss God Himself. That makes me wonder why more Christians are not reading it every day!

Through my 50 years as a Christian, I have seen the impact of the Bible on my life and of so many other people.

---

[68] II Timothy 3:16 NAS
[69] I Corinthians 13:12
[70] Isaiah 40:8
[71] Hebrews 4:12
[72] John 14:27
[73] Timothy 3:17

Since the Bible is God's Word, we should cherish it by studying, obeying, sharing it with others, and fully trusting every part of it as truth.

TRUTH ABOUT VEGETABLE AND MEAT PROTEIN

God's word is the truth, even when it comes to what we eat. In creation in Genesis 1:29, God tells Adam that he has given him all plants that yield seed and fruit trees to be his food. In Genesis 9:3, God tells Noah that after the flood waters subside, He will give him every moving thing that is alive for his food and as well the green plants given to him previously. However, in Daniel 1:12-16 he proved to the king that they could be vegetarian and still be as healthy and strong as the king's men. Everything God made for us to eat is good. I'm going to write about what is most beneficial for our health.

It is a common misunderstanding that dietary protein is only obtained through animal sources like chicken, beef, fish, and dairy. However, nuts, seeds, legumes, rice, grains, vegetables, mushrooms, and especially dark green leafy vegetables are considerable sources of dietary protein, too. Protein plays an important role in numerous bodily functions and is an important part of a balanced diet. It is also important to keep our pH balanced according to the food we eat. You can search for food charts that list Acid & Alkaline foods. It is recommended that 80% of the food we eat should be alkali. You will see that meat and all higher protein foods are acidic, and most vegetables, especially dark greens, are alkali-forming foods in our bodies. Unfortunately, our Canadian diets include meat as the center of our meals, which causes a more acidic condition in the body that causes inflammation and disease. There are plenty of reasons to eat less meat in your meals, such as cheaper to make, lower in calories, and more health benefits.

People might ask if vegetable protein is a complete protein. The term complete protein refers to amino acids, which are the building blocks of protein. There are 20 different amino acids that can form a protein; of those, nine can't be made by the body. These are called essential amino acids, which we need to get from the food we eat to provide what we need for our bodies. To be considered a complete protein, it must contain all nine of these essential amino acids in roughly equal amounts. You can combine the right types of food to ensure you get complete protein in your vegetarian meal. I find it easy to remember what foods complete a vegetarian meal: add a green, grain and a bean or another high-protein vegetable instead of beans with each meal. Some other vegetables besides beans that are high in protein are peas, shitake mushrooms, artichokes, avocado, nuts, and seeds. You can always Google high protein vegetables to see how many grams of protein are in each vegetable per serving. The National Academy of Medicine says that we need 7 grams of protein daily for every 20 pounds of body weight. The main sources of B-12 are meat, eggs, and dairy, and other sources of plant-based milk, fortified cereal, and nutritional yeast are other sources. Most vegetarians like me, will still eat some eggs and dairy. You can take 1,000 mcg of a B-12 sublingual to dissolve under your tongue daily to ensure you get enough in your diet. Since I'm anemic, taking two 5,000 mcg a day of B-12 plus a natural iron supplement and extra vitamin C is recommended since iron is difficult for the body to absorb. There is no concern about the build-up of toxins because B-12 is water soluble.

Dr. Joel Fuhrman, ND, explains the benefits of plant-based protein in his book Eat to Live. Doctor Fuhrman explains that when you compare calories to calories, plant sources provide the same amount of protein as animal sources, and in many cases, even more! For example, Dr. Fuhrman's study shows that 100 calories of broccoli contain 11 grams of protein, while 100 calories of steak contain only 6 grams of protein. Not only does broccoli contain protein, but it also provides a significant amount of fiber, phytochemicals, calcium, and antioxidants. Steak provides none of those nutrients and contains cholesterol and saturated fat. There is another aspect of eating meat from Dr. Peter D'Adamo in a book he has written called *"Eat Right for Your Blood Type."* He has done medical and genetic research, which reveals that blood type is the key to your biochemical uniqueness. Without getting into full details, O & A blood types are the most common in people. The O blood type are the only ones who can digest beef successfully, and the A blood type should be vegetarian. I know from being an A blood type that I never have digested meat well. I had a client with an O blood type who didn't feel well when she tried to be a vegetarian. For those who need to eat meat, it is still wise to eat small portions of organic meat and larger portions of organic vegetables. Organic food is always the best choice for getting more nutrients with no harmful chemicals, which helps support a healthier body.

A diet with large amounts of meat can make you sleepy, give you brain fog, constipation, harm our heart, cause inflammation in the body, weight gain, colon cancer, and are more likely to produce kidney stones. Hopefully, this will help you to understand how vegetables are an important part of your diet since they are nutrient-rich with vitamins, minerals, antioxidants, and fiber. A diet with various vegetables also keeps inflammation down, balances blood pressure, eye health, healthy skin, healthy heart, balanced blood sugar levels, brain health, stronger immunity, and cancer-fighting nutrients.

THIS COULD CHANGE EVERYTHING

"The peace of God, which surpasses all comprehension, shall guard your hearts and your minds in Christ Jesus."

Philippians 4:7

What does it mean to have peace that surpasses all understanding? Wouldn't it be nice not to worry when facing challenging times? We are going to discover how this is possible through prayer.

When we accept Jesus into our lives, we receive direct access to our Heavenly Father because Jesus replaced the job of the priest.[74] Matthew 6:8 tells us God already knows our needs before we pray, but God wants us to talk with Him about everything in prayer every day so we can keep that personal relationship with Him. This makes it a privilege to be able to come before God to talk about our needs and concerns. We usually come to God to tell Him our problems and ask Him to change the circumstances. The primary purpose of prayer is not always to change our circumstances but to trust that God knows what is best for us and that we can change for good through the process. King David said in Psalms 34:4, "I sought the Lord, and He answered me, and delivered me from all my fears." David did not say that God took him out of his circumstances, but instead, God delivered him from his fears of the circumstances. We often are fearful or anxious about things we have no control over. When we hang on to our fears, it robs us of our peace. Philippians

---

[74] Hebrews 4:14-15

4:6 says to "be anxious for nothing" but let your request be known to God.

In the Lord's Prayer, Jesus gives us a pattern of what our prayers should include.[75] First, in verse 9, we recognize that we are praying to God with an intimate title, *"Our Father in heaven."* This relates to the privileged relationship with God as our father, which we share with the community of believers in Christ. We also express praise by acknowledging God's holiness. Verse 10 is asking us to pray for God's Kingdom to come to earth so then His will is final in heaven and earth. The kingdom of God that is on earth now is the born-again believers that are the light of the world to show others Jesus, also know known as the Body of Christ. In verse 11, we ask God to provide for our daily needs, things like food, shelter, and clothing. In Verse 12, we ask for forgiveness of our own sins while recognizing that we need to forgive others as well. In verse 13, we ask God for deliverance so that we will not fall away from Him when we are being tempted by Satan. Then, the verse ends with praise for God's greatness forever. The emphasis on sin continues in verses 14-15 about the importance of forgiving others because God has forgiven us. Also, keep in mind that all our sins are forgiven past, present, and future through the death of Christ on the cross.[76] However, we can still be tempted and decide to sin, which causes divisions in our relationship with God. God is Holy and cannot be a part of sin, so when we do sin then we ask God for forgiveness of that sin to continue our close relationship.[77] We know that God does not tempt us, but when we are tempted by Satan in our areas of weakness, it is not beyond what we can handle because God will even provide a way

---

[75] Matthew 6:9-15 NAS
[76] Hebrews 10:12-14
[77] I John 1:9, Psalm 66:18

of escape.[78] The prayer begins and ends with *praise,* which not only glorifies God but reminds us how great He is in our minds and our hearts. Then, we can focus on the resources of God and not our problems, which will allow us to lay hold of God's will that He might be glorified.

Jesus also talks about prayer when describing Himself as the vine and his people as the branches.[79] In this illustration, Jesus is saying we need to stay in a constant relationship with Him to stay connected to Him. With Jesus as our life source, we are praying in His name to receive the promise of answered prayers. We stay connected to Jesus not only in prayer but also in reading the Bible and in fellowship with other believers. In Philippians, it tells us that God does not only answer big prayers but also tells us to pray about everything. Sometimes, we overlook the everyday answers to prayer as if they just happened. In I Thessalonians 5:17, it says, "pray without ceasing" which means we are talking to God throughout the day and not just in prayer time. I believe that having a prayer mindset throughout the day also helps us to take "every thought captive" and give it to God.[80] God is not a genie that gives us everything we want when we want it because God's plans and timing are different than ours.[81] When we do not see an immediate change in our hardship, we feel our prayers and cries to God are not being heard. Did you know that most of the time when we pray, there is a spiritual battle going on that can delay your answer to a prayer? We see an example of this when Daniel was in captivity. Throughout his time in captivity, he was continually praying about his concerns. Then, one day, an angel appeared to Daniel and told

---

[78] James 1:13, I Corinthians 10:12-13
[79] John 15:5-7,
[80] II Corinthians 10:5 NAS
[81] Psalm 90:4, Isaiah 55: 8-, John 15:5-7

him God heard his prayers, but there was a spiritual battle happening to defeat an evil angel[82] Jesus even told the disciples a parable in Matthew 7:1-5 that related to the importance of persistence in prayer. Even though there are various things that can hinder our prayers, the Bible tells us in I John 5:14, "This is the confidence we have before Him, if we ask anything according to *His will*, He hears us." We are in His will if we are abiding in Jesus.

We can trust God's word regarding His promises for prayer. As we give everything to God in *prayer,* we will have peace that surpasses all comprehension as we leave it with Him.

Keep on believing God hears and do not stop praying!

---

[82] Danielle 10:11-13

CHANGE ANXIETY & DEPRESSION

It says in the Bible to be anxious for nothing and to cast your cares on the Lord. Only Jesus can truly give you comfort and peace in life's most difficult challenges. Let us look at some health issues that are the effects of anxiety and depression.

The definition in the Oxford dictionary of anxiety is a feeling of worry, nervousness, or unease, which usually is about an upcoming event or something with an uncertain outcome. With anxiety, we all feel that occasionally in various situations, but it becomes a concern if it continues all the time. They call depression a mental health disorder, but we can all have intense sadness, which includes feeling helpless, hopeless, and worthless sometimes. However, just like anxiety, if it continues, it can be hard to leave those feelings. It seems to me that everything is based on cause and effect in any health condition. If there is a deep-rooted hurt, abuse, or tragedy in someone's life, they should seek counseling or it will only get worse, and then the person will be prescribed medication which only mask the cause. It is common for someone with an anxiety disorder to also suffer from depression or vice versa. About one-half of those diagnosed with depression were also diagnosed with an anxiety disorder. The National Institute of Mental Health state that depression is most common in ages 18 to 25, and women are twice as likely as men to suffer from it.

There are several reasons that you can suffer from Anxiety and Depression. We are going to look at some of the natural things that happen within the body to try to understand why and know what you can do to help. Anxiety can be due to hormonal imbalance, which might be caused by an imbalance in the endocrine system.

The endocrine system plays a key role in our emotional state, by regulating energy levels, helps to deal with stress and keeps us calm. When this hormonal system gets out of balance, there are symptoms of anxiety, depression, irritability, mood swings, foggy brain, tense muscles, and sleep disturbances that can occur. Our adrenal glands participate in making numerous hormones for normal functioning, such as blood sugar regulation, producing and maintaining the body's energy levels in conjunction with the thyroid, and producing stress-monitoring hormones. Since the adrenals contribute to about 35 percent of premenopausal female hormones and almost 50 percent of postmenopausal hormones, it can compromise the adrenal function profoundly which will affect hormonal balance. Dealing with stress is another major cause of anxiety. In response to stress, our body produces adrenaline, which can cause anxiety. The extra drain of adrenaline from the adrenals causes such things as chronic fatigue, fibromyalgia, or both. The thyroid cannot function by itself because it works in conjunction with other endocrine organs like the adrenals, pituitary, pancreas, liver, and reproductive organs. The thyroid needs to work harder when organs such as the liver or adrenal glands are overworked or overstimulated by stress, food allergies, poor diet, and or lack of sleep. Then anxiety could be a result of either an overactive or underactive thyroid. In people with depression, the levels of certain brain chemicals can be out of balance, particularly these neurotransmitters: serotonin (which regulates mood, emotion, and sleep), dopamine (which affects movement, attention, and feelings of pleasure), and norepinephrine (which regulate arousal, sleep, attention, and mood). These are a few ideas of what the body might be lacking that could result in suffering from Anxiety and Depression. You can request a test for your adrenal, thyroid, and hormones to check and see if there is an imbalance. I have a friend who would get so anxious that he could not leave his house. He went to a Naturopath, which sent him to a chelation therapist to be evaluated for heavy metals in his body. There was a high count of lead in his body, which was the cause of the problem. They were able to help through chelation therapy. Another friend of mine had her baby girl die at eight months old. She suffered from severe anxiety to the point she could not go anywhere or do anything to live a normal life. When she went for a check up by her Naturopath, they found it was adrenal exhaustion caused by the tragic experience of losing her baby. They put her on high doses of licorice root and other supplements to support the adrenals and it helped her to heal. These are two examples of similar symptoms but different causes, so it is always wise to search out the cause.

After you find out the cause, in most cases, the best thing is to take control of your health by first starting to eat healthier. Stay away from things such as fast food, fruit juices, regular & diet pop, energy drinks, coffee, alcohol, white refined flours, bread, donuts, pastries, ketchup, artificial sweeteners, products made with hydrogenated oils, crackers, chips, processed meats, red meats, wheat, and dairy. The best choices of things to eat are mostly gluten-free or sprouted grain bread, fiber-rich grains, fruits (no acidic), vegetables, dark greens, good fats, and dark chocolate (with natural sugars). It will be helpful to also search for a healthy, natural diet plan.

More doctors are realizing that the colon plays a significant role in mental health too. They have even found children with learning disabilities are low in friendly bacteria in the gut. Things that can destroy friendly bacteria in the gut for children are medications, vaccinations, bad eating habits, and consumption of excess refined foods and sweet snacks. To help build up your family's digestive tract it is important to make healthy choices in how you eat, taking a good fiber supplement and a probiotic every day. Also, it is important to nourish the brain, nerves, adrenals, and make sure you are getting enough sleep. Supplement suggestions for stress and anxiety are Magnesium, L-theanine (Mental Calm), Fish Oils high in DHA, Vitamin D 1,000 IU emulsified drops, B6 plus a Vitamin B-100 complex, GABA, Ashwagandha and Licorice Root (not if diabetic). You can visit your local Health Food Store for suggestions for these products.

DO NOT BE AFRAID

"God has not given us a spirit of fear, but of power, love, and discipline."

II Timothy 1:7

In the Bible, the word fear is written 500 times and included in that is the phrase "fear not" or "do not be afraid," which is quoted 365 of those times. God knows we are fearful people, and that may be why it written about so many times in the Bible. We all have known fear at various times in our lives and in different forms. What is true fear, and why do we experience it?

When it comes to fear there are three basic types of fear. The *first fear* is an *emotion* that God gave us for protection when we think our lives are at risk. When we are *scared*, our body produces a chemical called adrenaline that flows throughout our body and works as a stimulus that causes the fight or flight response. One example of that in the Bible is I Kings 19:1-3, when Elijah had to run for his life from Jezebel since she had ordered him to be killed. The *second fear* is different than the others because it is *respect* for God because of His awesome power. In Proverbs 9:10 it says, "The fear of the Lord is the beginning of wisdom," which is the fear that comes when we understand who God is through His word. We learn of His power in the world plus in our life, and that gives us a greater respect for Him. The *third* fear happens when we think about the worst-case scenario in *circumstances*, which allows fear to dictate our behavior instead of trusting God. A fitting example of this is after a long day of ministry, Jesus got into the boat with his disciples to reach the other side. Jesus fell asleep in the boat then a storm came upon them, and the disciples were afraid for their life. Instead of trusting Jesus and asking for help, they assumed the worst that He did not care. After Jesus calmed the storm, He questioned their lack of faith. The disciples had been with Jesus every day to see many miracles performed, but they were still afraid, even with Him in the boat. It seems clear they did not completely understand who Jesus was because after the miracle, they questioned each other about His power.[83] Do we fully understand and trust the power we have with Jesus in our life?

It has even proven in our lives that we have the natural fear to protect our life. In the Bible we says to fear (respect) God. However, the third fear that we all struggle with is like the disciples, which Jesus considered a lack of faith. Some practical examples of this in our life is that we fear what *people* will think of us when we want to share our faith. The Bible assures us that even if man says things against us or even kills us, he cannot take away our salvation.[84] Our part is to share our faith whenever possible and trust God with the results because what do we have to lose? We fear having the *material things* we need even though God says He will take care of all our needs.[85] We also fear when we are uncertain of our *purpose* or *direction* in life, so we need faith to trust that God can lead and guide us.[86] We can fear the *future* because of circumstances that have come into our lives that bring change, with an uncertain outcome. Since God is good, so are His plans to help us through the

---

[83] Mark 4:35-41
[84] John 10:28-29
[85] Matthew 6:25-33
[86] Proverbs 3:5-6

circumstances of life, that will lead us to what is best for our life now and in the future.[87]

Paul's faith was a great example of how God gave him courage in ministry. When Paul met Jesus in Acts chapter 9 on the road to Damascus it dramatically changed his life. Even though we may not all have a dramatic testimony like Paul, God can take everyone's life and change it forever.[88] Paul was not perfect and had his own personal struggles, just like we do. In Philippians 4:13, Paul says, "I can do all things through Him who strengthens me." Paul's trust in God gave him a strong faith and a passionate commitment to his ministry so that he was not overcome by fear. As we know, in Paul's ministry, he faced many dangers, such as being beaten, thrown in prison, shipwrecks, bitten by a venomous snake, and standing in front of many officials who wanted to put him to death. The fears we face may never be anything like Paul's, but no matter how big or small our ministry is, in our home, neighborhood, church, or mission field, there probably will be times we will face certain fears. Then, we need to make a choice whether to put our trust in God or fear our circumstances.

Faith is our antidote for fear because, as it tells us in Hebrews 11:6, "without faith it is impossible to please God. Since our relationship with the Father, Son, and Holy Spirit are based on an active faith, II Corinthians 5:7 says, "we are to walk by faith and not by sight." In Philippians 4:8, Paul reminds us to think of what is good, so we do not dwell on bad things which can cause fear. When we fear certain situations, we have the promise in Romans 8:28, "We know that God

---

[87] Jeremiah 29:11
[88] II Corinthian 5:17

causes all things to work together for good to those who love God, to those called according to His purpose." That does not mean that He will do exactly what we think should be done for our good, but we should trust that God will do what is ultimately best for us from His perspective of eternity.[89]

In I John 4:18, it says, "There is no fear in love, but perfect love cast out fear," so we can rest in God's perfect love and not be fearful.

---

[89] Isaiah 55:8-9, Jeremiah 29:11-13

STRESSED ADRENAL GLANDS

When I wrote the devotion on fear, it was mentioned that God had placed the adrenal glands in our body as a form of protection. When in danger, the adrenal glands secrete a hormone called adrenaline that increases the rate of blood circulation, breathing, and carbohydrate metabolism to prepare muscles for exertion. This is known as the "fight or flight mechanism," which means the body is preparing to fight to survive against an opponent or take flight in the fastest way possible to safety. We don't often think about the adrenals and the importance they play in our total health.

There are two Adrenal Glands in which there is one over top of each kidney. The adrenal glands are involved in several functions in the body. They participate in pulmonary functions, blood sugar metabolism, carbohydrate metabolism, central nervous system processes, cardiovascular function, hormone production, gastrointestinal function, and liver function. The adrenal glands produce hormones along with two structures in the brain, which are called the hypothalamus and the pituitary gland. The adrenal glands, via these hormones, control many functions, from anti-inflammatory (clear the body of pain and swelling), immune system protection, balances fluid plus salt levels, controlling minerals (such as calcium & potassium), rapid heart rate, regulating blood pressure, sleep, and wake cycles. They even function as backup organs producing estrogen during and after menopause.

When you experience stress of any kind, the adrenals start pumping adrenaline, cortisol, and other adrenal hormones. These hormones get blood flowing to the heart and muscles and, at the same time, pull the blood away from your digestion. They also stimulate the nervous system to speed up the heart rate and prepare your body for stress. Every type of stress plus trauma influences these glands, such as injury, infection, divorce, finances, job-related stress, irritable people, drugs, medications, surgery (even dental), pain, illness, poison ivy, extreme cold or heat, giving birth, menstrual cycle, staring at computer monitors, eating junk foods, starvation diets, etc. When stress and poor nutrition lead to altered hormone levels, an imbalance in endocrine function can lead to substantial fatigue. The emotional stress of the loss of a loved one is 1,000 times more than any other form of stress to deplete the adrenals.

As you push your body over the years to cope with stress, living on caffeine, nicotine, sugar, and alcohol with little sleep, the adrenals eventually become exhausted. In this state, the adrenals cannot function like they need to. When the stress goes on too long, or the body is exposed to excess shock and stress, you lose the ability to adapt to the stress, or the body stays in this stress mode when no stress is present, which becomes anxiety problems. This is called Adrenal fatigue or burnout, which can create other health concerns, such as autoimmune disorders like chronic fatigue and fibromyalgia. Also, the adrenal glands cause fat to accumulate in the belly as a survival protection mechanism in attempts to store future energy (fat) for the vital organs.

There are some things you can do naturally to support your Adrenals. Timing your meals is important to help regulate your blood sugar levels, which support the adrenal glands. Eat breakfast and eat regularly throughout the day. Skipping breakfast and lunch forces your body to burn stored nutrients and reduces your energy level. When you eat regular, balanced meals and healthy snacks, you can support your energy and cortisol levels all day. Also, it helps you to remain hydrated because dehydration can influence your stress levels and force your adrenal glands to produce cortisol. It is good to eat high protein foods, vegetables (especially green leafy vegetables), good fats, and whole grains to increase your energy levels naturally so you do not burn stored nutrients. Foods to avoid are refined sugar, refined flour, alcohol, caffeine, pop, fried foods, processed foods, fast foods, and artificial sweeteners.

If the adrenals are drained that means your vitamin C is already depleted. So, you will need a buffered Vitamin C, which will allow you to take larger amounts, from 4,000 – 10,000 mg a day. It is safe to take up to 10,000mg because Vitamin C is water soluble and will flush out what you don't need. I take a powdered form in which ¼ teaspoon equals 1,000 mg which makes it an easier form to take higher doses and add to drinks or smoothies. You need vitamin B-100 Complex to help the stress load on the body. You will need to take a B Complex with 1 capsule two times a day. Other B Vitamins that are needed are B5 and B6, which you can take with your B complex. B Complex is water soluble, so it won't build up toxins in the body. Individual B vitamins are not water soluble, so they should always be taken with a B complex to help them break down. I would also suggest a B-12 sublingual 5,000 mcg 1 tablet two times a day in a clear mouth, which will give you more energy. Other supplements for the adrenals are Ashwagandha, L-Theanine, and magnesium, which help control stress levels and support healthy adrenals.

THE BATTLE BELONGS TO GOD

"Put on the full armour of God, that you may be able to stand firm against the schemes of the devil."

Ephesians 6:11

In Ephesians 6:12, Paul tells the Christians that the battle is beyond flesh and blood because it is a spiritual battle. Our battle is in a realm that we cannot see, which includes different ranks of evil forces fighting against good. We need to believe in and understand the battle we are enduring daily since it occurs regardless of whether we choose to engage in it, since it is completely a different level of fighting. God has given us spiritual armour that is invisible to protect us from forces of evil that want to separate our close relationship with Him. To make our spiritual armour relatable, Paul gives us a comparison of the warrior's armour they used for the body when they went to battle. We do not see our enemy or realize why we are in battle, like in an earthly battle. This makes it more important to always be prepared because "Satan prowls about like a roaring lion, seeking someone to devour."[90] We use our spiritual armour to fight a daily battle to protect our spiritual life, but we are not fighting the battle for our salvation because that battle was won at the cross.[91]

We still use a form of armour in the military now for protection, but it looks different. Ephesians 6:14-18 lists the armour of God and the purpose of each piece. Paul lists the parts of the armour in the order

---

[90] 1 Peter 5:8 NAS
[91] 1 John 5:11-13

that the soldier would have put them on, which will also reflect the importance of safety in each area of our body for spiritual battle. The *first* piece of armour listed is the *belt of truth*. The armour belt was very thick and held the breastplate on, plus held the sheath, which was the holder for the sword. When we hold onto God's truth in His promises, it holds everything together for us in battle.[92] Since Satan is the father of lies, he cannot stand against our belief in God's truth that we are free.[93] The *second* piece of armour is the *breastplate of righteousness, which* covers the heart and other vital organs that give us life. We accept Jesus with our heart as our personal savior which covers us with righteousness so we can live right before God. This protection enables us to defeat Satan from harming our spiritual life.[94] The *third* piece of armour is to cover our *feet with the gospel of peace*. Soldiers would wear protective footwear to allow them to stand firm in battle. Since the gospel is our salvation through Jesus, it allows us to stand firm because God gives peace to us through eternal security.[95] The Bible also says beautiful are the feet when we go tell others the good news.[96] We defeat Satan as we share the gospel of peace by bringing others into God's kingdom away from Satan's grip. The *fourth* piece of armour is the *shield of faith*. A shield was made of wood or metal and protected a soldier's body from incoming projectiles and injury from close combat. It also could be used to extinguish flaming arrows that were fired by the enemy. Our shield of faith also gives us extra safety and security in what Jesus has done for us. Our faith can extinguish the lies of the devil as he attacks us with distractions, trials, and unbelief.[97]

---

[92] John 8:31-36
[93] John 8:44
[94] Romans 10:9-10
[95] John 3:16
[96] Romans 10:14-15, 1 Peter 3:15
[97] II Corinthians 10:4-5

The *fifth* piece of armour is the *helmet of salvation*. Helmets were and continue to be a vital piece of protection for the brain during battle. The primary battlefield in spiritual warfare is in the Christian's mind. Satan likes to attack us through our thoughts to whisper doubts, especially about our salvation, and we have the assurance of God's promises that will shed truth on Satan's lies.[98] The final weapon in our arsenal is the *sword of the spirit*, which is God's word. This is our offensive weapon in the battle of spiritual warfare. Christians have the power to defeat Satan when we quote God's word to him.[99] Jesus used this method of attack when he was in the desert, tempted by Satan.[100] Since it is important to use our defense, we need to accomplish that by being in His word every day.[101]

It is good to know the strengths and weaknesses of your enemy and his tactics. Satan will attack us in our areas of weakness so he can steal our joy, hope, and peace. These strategies make us feel like we are living a defeated life, plus divide churches, families, and marriages. Even though the spiritual armour is important for our protection, we need to "pray at all times in the Spirit" for ourselves and others.[102] We should praise God for who He is and have confidence in His power through our prayers. Paul's life was a notable example of this, as the authorities tried to keep Paul from spreading the good news about Jesus. Although, even in prison He praised and prayed with the confidence that God was in control.

We need to be on the alert every day for battle, but remember, *"Greater is He that is in you than he that is in the world."*[103]

---

[98] 1 John 5:11-13, John 10:27-29
[99] Hebrews 4:12
[100] Matthew 4:4-11
[101] Psalm 119:11, II Timothy 3:16-17
[102] Ephesians 6:18 NAS
[103] I John 4:4 NAS

LYMPHATIC SYSTEM ARMOR

In our faith, we must fight off the enemy with our spiritual armor, and to keep our body strong, we need to keep up our defense in our Lymphatic System. We live in a fallen world that puts us in a spiritual struggle to keep strong in our faith, and there are also things we need to fight off that destroy our bodies. God has given us an Immune System to be our defense, so let's look at ways to help keep that defense up.

The Lymphatic system is the body's inside armor for the protection of our health. It is a vital part of the immune system that includes the Thymus Gland, Bone Marrow, Spleen, Tonsils, Appendix, and Peyer's Patches (in small intestines), as well as a network of lymph nodes connected by lymphatic vessels. This system transports lymph throughout the body.

Lymph is formed from fluids that seeps through the thin walls of the capillaries into the body tissues. This fluid contains oxygen, proteins, and other nutrients that nourish the tissue. Some of these fluids re-enter capillaries, and some of it enters the lymphatic vessels, which become lymph. Small lymphatic vessels connect to larger ones and eventually form the thoracic duct. The thoracic duct is the largest lymphatic vessel, which joins with the subclavian vein and returns lymph to the bloodstream. Lymph also transports foreign substances such as bacteria, cancer cells, and dead or damaged cells that may be present in tissues into the lymphatic vessels and to the lymph organs for disposal. The lymph holds many white blood cells that are formed in the bone and are our fighters for defending the body from infectious diseases and foreign invaders. All substances transported by the lymph pass through at least one lymph node, where foreign substances can be filtered out and destroyed before fluid is returned to the bloodstream. In the lymph nodes, white blood cells can collect, interact with each other and with antigens, and generate immune responses to foreign substances. Lymph nodes contain a mesh of tissue that is tightly packed with B cells and T cells. Harmful microorganisms are filtered through the mesh, then found and attacked by B cells and T cells. Lymph nodes are often clustered in areas where the lymphatic vessels branch off, such as the neck, armpits, and groin.

These are helpful tips to promote healthy lymphatic system functions with a proper diet and healthy habits.

Avoid cow dairy, gluten, sugar, and other processed foods because these choices clog the flow & lead to congestion.

Eat leafy greens, herbs, fruits, more plant foods will make it easier for intestinal fluids to move to the lymph nodes.

Hydrate regularly to get enough fluid to keep lymphatic flow from getting sluggish.

Massage or skin brush because lymph nodes are just below the surface of the skin, and this helps to stimulate the flow. Always massage and skin brush toward the heart.

Reduce stress because it can cause sluggish lymphatic flow too.

Exercise is good, especially jumping on a rebounder because it pumps the circulation upward for better flow throughout the body.

You can also take supplements to cleanse and help the lymph flow, such as vitamins C and D, zinc, garlic, milk thistle, burdock, and turmeric. There is also a drainage cream called Lymphdiaral, which you apply around the area of the nodes with light movements toward the heart. For women, it is especially important to concentrate under the armpits and around the breast.

Just google a Lymphatic System chart and print it off. This will help you understand better where the Lymphatic System is throughout your body. This will also help for massaging the skin for lymphatic flow too.

FREEDOM

"It was for freedom that Christ set us free; therefore, keep standing firm and do not be subject again to a yoke of slavery."

Galatians 5:1

Jesus tells us that everyone who commits sin is a slave to sin but that He can set us free.[104] When we accept Jesus into our lives, we are free from the bondage of sin. How, then, can a Christian become entangled in sin again? We are told in Hebrews to get all obstacles and sin set aside so we do not become entangled in them.[105] Let's look in the Bible to see the sin and the obstacles that entangle us and our part to stay connected to that freedom.

When Paul wrote his letter to the Romans, he wanted to correct an error of doctrine that had crept into the church regarding sin. They believed that if they increased in their sin, grace might increase. Paul told them emphatically that was not true, and then he told them why they did not need to sin to receive more grace. He explained God's grace was shown to us through Christ's death to allow us to die to sin, which enabled us to no longer be a slave to sin.[106] God continues to show us grace by giving us the opportunity to escape sin when we are being tempted.[107] If we foster the things that lead to the temptation to sin, it tells us in I John 1:9 that He gives us the opportunity to repent. There are various kinds of sin we may get entangled in, but all sin is against God because we are

---

[104] John 8:34-36
[105] Hebrews 12:1
[106] Romans 6:11-16
[107] I Corinthians 10:13

violating God's commands that He has given to protect us. However, now, we are no longer under the bondage of sin, but sin becomes a choice as we become obedient to God through His word.

We can get entangled in religion, which focuses on man-made rules that enslave us to legalism. Galatians 4:1 says it was for freedom that Christ set us free, not to be subject to a yoke of slavery through religious rules that Jesus abolished with His death. Paul was concerned because the Galatians had been convinced by others that they needed to add religious laws to their faith in Christ. Paul confronted them with questions to help them see that their receiving the Spirit was not based on the law but on faith.[108] There are other false teachings that can creep in to entangle us, which sound good but are not true to God's word. A few years ago, our church congregation was surprised and saddened when an active couple in our church became entangled in a faith of hyper-grace. They found a website in which a pastor was promoting that Christians live by grace, so there is no need for communion, baptism, and confession of our sins because that was for then, and now Christians live by Paul's teachings. They tried to convince other members of our church, too, so they were asked by leadership to leave the church. Paul tells us to destroy speculations, and everything raised up against the knowledge of God.[109] Jesus tells us in John 8:31-32 if you abide in His word, then you are truly a believer, and you will know the truth that will make you free. When you are having trouble understanding the scripture, it says in James 1:5, ask God for wisdom because He will give it to us. Then God can use several ways to do that, such as by giving you a better understanding as you continue to read His word or, a message from a pastor, or spiritual insight from a mature Christian.

---

[108] Galatians 3:1-5
[109] II Corinthians 10:5

In I John 2:16, John gives a description of worldly things that we can get entangled in. *Lust of the flesh* which is a lack of moderation for things that satisfy the body, like food, strong drink, and drugs. *Lust of the eyes,* which is never being satisfied with enough possessions. *Boastful pride of life,* which is desiring honor for your own accomplishments. Jesus teaches in Matthew 6:24 that no one can serve two masters, like God and riches, or he will find one more important than the other. As we know, the Bible does not say money is evil; it is only if the love of money takes the place of God, who should be the most important thing in our lives. Jesus also says in Matthew 6:21 "for where your treasure is, so will your heart be also." This can include anything that becomes more important than God and building His kingdom. God has given us His Holy Spirit to help us overcome all these worldly things each day. If we walk by the Spirit, as it says in Galatians 5:16, then we will not carry out the desires of the flesh.

God wants a relationship with us and has, therefore, given us the freedom to choose. When we sin, it is an active choice to go against God's character and to suffer the consequences. As born-again Christians, we receive God's forgiveness of all our sins, past, present, and future. We have become free from sin and now desire to serve God. When we become free from sin, we have the benefit of being holy and receiving the promise of eternal life.[110] We become children of God and get to be lavished with His love.[111] We can choose to be obedient to God's word and dependent on the Holy Spirit as our Helper to experience our true freedom.

Since we have experienced God's love, which gives us true freedom, why would we want to be subject again to a yoke of slavery?

---

[110] Romans 6:22
[111] I John 3:1

BREATHE FREE RESPIRATORY SYSTEM

Spiritual breathing is important to staying free in the Spirit. In Spiritual breathing each day we exhale any known sins or wrongful attitudes or actions and we inhale by inviting God to rule in our hearts for the day. Just as important as spiritual breathing is to our spiritual life, so is having the freedom to breathe with a healthy Respiratory System. Both are similar because you breathe in the good and exhale the bad.

We know the Respiratory System enables us to breathe, but here are the basic details of how it works. The respiratory tract conveys air from the mouth and nose to the lungs, where oxygen and carbon dioxide are exchanged between the alveoli and the capillaries. The lungs are a gas-exchanging organ, where its delicate tissues are protected by the bony and muscular chest cavity. The lung provides the tissues of the human body with a continuous flow of oxygen and clears the blood of the gaseous waste product, carbon dioxide. Atmospheric air pressure is pumped in and out regularly through a system of pipes called conducting airways, which join the gas exchange region with the outside of the body. The airways are divided into upper and lower since they are both involved in breathing. The upper consists of the nose, mouth, sinuses, pharynx (upper section of the throat), and the larynx (voice box). The lower airway system consists of the trachea (windpipe), the stem bronchi (bronchial tubes), and all the airways go within the lungs. The diaphragm is the major muscle that lies at the base of the rib cage, which enables you to inhale and exhale. The intercostal muscles of the chest are external and internal, which are groups of muscles that run between the ribs that help form and move the chest wall. They work together with the central nervous system to provide sensory information to the respiratory center of the brain for the pumping action of the lungs. The blood is a carrier for gases, and the Circulatory System (heart & blood vessels) are mandatory elements for a working Respiratory System.

Chronic respiratory diseases are one of the leading causes of death. Diseases that are associated with the respiratory system include chronic obstructive pulmonary disease, emphysema, bronchitis, tuberculosis, pneumonia, and asthma. Ways to keep your lungs healthy are by not smoking, exercising, eating a healthy diet, avoiding outdoor pollution exposure, improving indoor air quality, and deep breathing exercises. Suggested vitamins that can help keep the Respiratory System healthy are A, B-12, C, D, and E to fend off respiratory infections. Vitamins A, D and E are fat-soluble vitamins that can build up toxins in the body if you take higher doses. However, you can buy A and D in an emulsified formula for better absorption and no toxic build up. You can also get B-12 sublingual chews that you absorb under your tongue to get better absorption. They are water-soluble and have no toxic build-up in the body. Vitamin C is acidic unless taken in the form of Calcium Ascorbate (pH balanced), and the best natural vitamin E source is Sunflower, which is a natural source of d-alpha tocopherol. If you have a compromised respiratory system, you can help keep it clear by eating an anti-inflammatory diet, which will help avoid producing excess mucous. This includes avoiding or limiting dairy, refined sugars, and flour and getting a completely anti-inflammatory diet plan. You can google it to put a copy on your fridge for quick reference.

My lungs had been compromised 17 years ago because of pneumonia. Since then, I found a few herbal remedies that have been a God send for me to keep my lungs clear. One of them is Mullein, which helps to strengthen the respiratory system and Lobelia drops, which relax the muscles and get rid of inflammation so you can breathe more freely. I also use a liquid herbal remedy called Respiractin, that I carry in my purse to help if I have trouble with a cough or breathing. You can also have a diffuser with essential oils of eucalyptus and peppermint in your home or bedroom at night. Breathing exercises can help, too, by removing the extra carbon dioxide in the lungs. You can do them by taking three quick breaths in through the nose and blowing out quickly through the mouth. Other supplements that are helpful are Folic Acid, Magnesium (powder best), Omega 3 Fish Oil, and Serrapeptase which can eliminate inflammation in the body and the lungs.

Hope these suggestions are helpful in giving you the freedom to breathe as it has for me!

TRUST AND OBEY

"Trust in the Lord with all your heart, and do not lean on your own understanding. In all your ways acknowledge Him, and He will make your path straight."

Proverbs 3:5-6

I remember a song from long ago that we often sang in church called Trust and Obey. The main verse was, "Trust and Obey, there is no other way, to be happy in Jesus, but to Trust and Obey." These words are so true for growth in our faith. In this study, we are going to discover different aspects of why we can trust God and why it is important to obey Him.

When I trust someone, it is usually a family member or friend because I believe they are honest, sincere, and will not deliberately do anything that will harm me. In the Oxford dictionary, the definition of *trust* is to have a firm belief in the reliability, truth, ability, or strength of someone or something. The definition of *faith* is the complete *trust* or confidence in someone, and the second definition of faith is a strong belief in God. So, basically, when you put your faith in God, you are saying you trust Him. To learn more about a person, you need to establish a relationship to build that trust. We may know about God, Jesus, and the Holy Spirit, but it has to go beyond just knowing who they are. Our first step is to trust that God is real, accept that God sent His son to die for our sins and receive the Holy Spirit as our helper in living the Christian life. We build that relationship of trust when we spend time reading the Bible to understand our relationship with God and prayer to build our communication. The Bible tells us God is trustworthy because

He cannot lie, and He does not change His mind like people.[112] Since God is eternal, so are His promises and the hope that goes with His promises. When you obey God, there are promises, such as you will be nourished to grow and bear fruit, you won't stumble in your faith, you will live a long life with peace, you will prosper, and you can have what you ask of God in prayer.[113]

In the Old Testament, two people who were great examples of trust and obedience to God were Abraham and Noah. They both believed in one God in spite of living in a time when there were many gods to worship. Then, because of their faith, God talked with them and gave them the responsibility to serve Him.[114] For Abraham, God asked him to leave his home for the Promised Land, and he was uncertain of where he would be traveling. However, it was because of Abraham's faith that he chose to trust and obey God and leave his home behind.[115] It was a strange request from God for Noah to build an arch since there had never been rain on the earth before. However, because of his faith in God, Noah trusted and obeyed God. Noah was persistent to carry out the mission that God had given him. His mission could have taken 50-75 years to complete all the instructions given to him to build the arch and collect all the animals.[116] Another time-consuming thing to do would have been to collect enough food for the animals plus get them set up in their rooms. We don't even think about all the time it would have taken to get all the food they would have to put together for Noah's family too.

In the Old Testament, they could talk to God but couldn't see Him directly, unless He appeared as the Angel of the Lord. God only gave

---

[112] Numbers 23:19
[113] Psalms 1:2-3, Psalm 119:165, Proverbs: 3:1-2, Proverbs 28:25, I John 3:22
[114] Hebrews 11:7-8
[115] Genesis 12:1-4
[116] Genesis 6:13-22

the spirit as needed, and they still had to live by the law. As Christians, we are so blessed because God gave us His son to die for us, as a pure and final sacrifice, which took away the burden that was required by the law to make sacrifices for sin. When we accept Jesus, God gives us the Holy Spirit to live within us as our helper, but we won't see God and Jesus till we are in heaven. We are living our personal faith by grace, but it is still important to trust and obey God. Hebrews 11:6 says, "without faith it is impossible to please Him, because he who comes to God must believe that He is, and that He is a rewarder to those who seek Him." We need to have faith to trust and obey even when it doesn't make sense as it was for Abraham and Noah.

Jesus was a great example of obedience to His father. As it says in Philippians 2:8, "He humbled Himself by becoming obedient to death, even death on the cross." Jesus tells the importance of obedience when He said, "He who has my commandments and keeps them, is he who loves me; and he who loves me will be loved by my father, and I will love him and disclose myself to him."[117] As it is recorded in the book of Acts, the disciples began their ministry after Jesus' death, resurrection, ascension to heaven, and then they had to wait for the Holy Spirit to come. Then in obedience they began to continue the mission that Jesus gave them to tell others about the Good News and make disciples.[118]

One time, as Peter was with the disciples on a mission to tell the good news, they were presented before the council. The high priest asked them why they were still preaching in Jesus' name when they were told not to, and they said, "we must obey God rather than man."[119] Paul says in Romans 6:16, "Do you not know when you

---

[117] John 14:21 NAS
[118] Acts 1:4-5, Matthew 28:18-20
[119] Acts 5:18-29 NAS

present yourself as slaves for obedience, you are slaves of the one whom you obey, either of sin resulting in death, or of obedience resulting in righteousness."

As Christians, we shouldn't have to trust and obey out of obligation but because of our love for Jesus and all He has done for us. With our faith in Jesus, we can enjoy all of God's promises when we Trust and Obey.

BALANCE YOUR pH

To trust and obey God takes faith that we will see results, as it similarly does to balance our pH. Just as we can not see our pH in the body, we can see results if we are actively involved in keeping it balanced.

The pH is the potential Hydrogen ions in the body. Hydrogen is the most abundant chemical element found in the universe, plus it is present in all bodily fluids, allowing toxins and waste to be transported and eliminated. With the help of hydrogen, joints in the body remain lubricated and able to perform their functions. The chemical parameter for the strength of acid-base is a pH value between 0 and 6 and an alkaline base pH value between 7-14. Any acidic number causes inflammatory conditions, and any extreme alkaline number over 7.5 causes rare diseases. The ideal alkaline number is 7-7.5, which would be in a pH-balanced body. The easiest way to figure out your alkaline-acid base is to measure the pH value of your urine. You can buy pH testing strips at your local Health Store. The most correct time to test is the 1st or 2nd urine of the morning before you have eaten. In the beginning, you can measure the pH value over a few days, taking notes of what you eat and drink, which will help to figure out what can be altering your pH levels. Then, as it improves, you can test it 1-2 times a week to make sure it is keeping balanced. It will take some changes in eating habits to get the pH balanced, which will not happen overnight. When you find your pH is not becoming balanced in the body, it might be that heavy metals have accumulated in the body. Heavy metals make the body acidic, which makes the body unable to keep a healthy pH, which causes disease. This can be determined by going to a Chelation Clinic to have a doctor test for heavy metals.

It is when humans eat and breathe that they gain energy for the body. Waste products arise in normal metabolism and are excreted by the body. If the body produces acidic metabolic waste products at a rate higher than it can be neutralized or excreted from the body, this will result in a hyper-acidity of the body in the long term. In cases of extensive lack of alkaline mineral salts and continuous hyper-acidity, the body resorts to using its own minerals to balance the pH. A few possible reasons for hyper-acidity are highly acidifying food such as processed food, refined sugars, flour, excess meat, insufficient air, and medications. Some of the best ways to alkalize the body are diet, exercise, sufficient fluids, and nutritional supplements.

In your daily meals, try to ensure you are eating 80% of alkalinizing foods. It would be helpful to do this by following a food chart that you can find on Google under alkaline-acid food chart, then print the chart and place it on the fridge as a guideline. Keep in mind that all meats are acidic, so always eat more vegetables than meat. Avoid or limit acidic fruits even though they are listed as alkaline, because they are extremely alkaline and will stir up acids in the body. It would normally be good to stir up the acids for the eliminative organs to remove them from the body. However, most people's eliminative organs are not functioning properly, so these fruits then cause inflammatory conditions in the body.

Regular exercise, such as walking or riding a bicycle, improves oxygen intake and promotes the release of carbonic acid in the form of carbon dioxide. If your health does not allow exercise, you can do low-impact exercise in the home or the backyard by doing stretches or palettes.

Take the recommended amount of fluid for your body type throughout the day. Water is always the best choice for hydrating and cleansing the body inside. Tap water is very acidic, so you can install a more balanced Reverse Osmosis (R.O.) purifying system under your sink. Reverse Osmosis is a good form of purified water but lacks minerals, so you can get mineral drops to put in each glass of water or purchase jugs of pH-balanced water.

You can use nutritional supplements, too, because it is not always easy to balance pH by diet alone. A couple of supplements that will help balance pH are a Green Food supplement (liquid or powder), calcium, magnesium, and a liquid mineral supplement or tissue salt tablets.

When we are actively involved in balancing our pH, it can help protect our body from colds, flu, and disease.

"But the fruit of the Spirit is love, joy, peace, patience, kindness, goodness, faithfulness, gentleness, self control; against such things there is no law"

Galatians 5:22-23

When we receive Jesus into our lives, the Holy Spirit comes in to fill us and helps us to display the fruit of the Spirit in our lives. The fruit of the Spirit is not plural because it comes from the characteristics of the one Spirit. As Christians, our lives are like a fruit tree in the growing season. This is because the Holy Spirit is developing Jesus' characteristics into our lives to bear fruit as we become more like Jesus and less like our old selves. We are going to look at the characteristics of the fruit of the Spirit to understand how God uses them in our Christian walk.

Love is Agape love that is unconditional, like God's love is for us.[120] Our human nature is to love with conditions, but as Christians, the Holy Spirit can give us this Agape love for others. In John 13:34-35, Jesus gave a new commandment to "love one another" as He has loved us, and people will know that we are His disciples because of our love for one another. *Joy* is only obtained through the hope we have in knowing God, believing in Jesus, and living our lives in dependence on the Holy Spirit.[121] Quite often, people think of joy and happiness as the same, but they are very different. Happiness is dependent on circumstances, but joy is a choice that we make to

---

[120] 1 Corinthians 13:4-7
[121] Romans 5:5, 15:13

experience it in all circumstances when we are trusting the Lord.[122] **Peace** is usually thought of as world peace, but Jesus said in John 14:27 that He gives true peace that is not like the world gives. World peace can never last because of a sinful world, but Jesus gives us peace that lasts through eternity. Since Jesus died on the cross, we can now come directly to God in prayer so that we can also experience "the peace of God, which surpasses all comprehension" when we give our concerns to God.[123] **Patience** is a difficult quality to have because of the instant gratification world we live in. Biblestudytools.com says patience implies suffering, enduring, or waiting as a determination of the will and not simply under necessity. It is easy to get angry or frustrated when things or people get in the way of plans. In Proverbs 14:29, it says, "Whoever is patient has great understanding, but one who is quick-tempered displays foolishness." Colossians 3:12-13 says to Christians that they are to "be patient with one another" and to forgive each other as God has forgiven us. Patience is also important for us as we wait on God's timing to complete His promises to us. **Kindness** is being considerate and showing compassion to others by doing and saying kind things. Jesus tells the disciples to be kind to one another, even in our forgiveness.[124] **Goodness** is described in Thayer's Greek Lexicon as an uprightness of heart and life. We are told not to lose heart in doing what is good and to be good to all people, especially to believers.[125] God is the author of goodness, and the Bible even reassures us in James 1:7 that "every good and perfect gift is from above." **Faithfulness** demonstrates loyalty, and God is always faithful to us, as it says in II Timothy 2:13. He is worthy of receiving our total commitment to Him and trusting in His promises. Some

---

[122] James 1:2-4
[123] Philippians 4:6-7 NAS
[124] Ephesians 4:32
[125] Galatians 6:9-10

examples of His promises of faithfulness are giving us hope for our salvation, helping in temptation, protecting us from the evil one, forgiving our sins, and that He is with us in our sufferings.[126] **Gentleness,** according to Baker's dictionary, is the sensitivity of disposition and kindness of behavior, founded on strength and prompted by love. Jesus was our example of gentleness when He was on earth by how He dealt with people, teaching and healing them and dealing even with sin like the woman caught in adultery.[127] In Matthew 11:29, Jesus tells us we can come to Him because He is "gentle and humble in heart," and He will give us rest. We can also use that gentleness when sharing our faith with others.[128] **Self-control** is basically control over our own emotions and behavior, especially in difficult situations. For the unbeliever, self-control can be used for their own selfishness, but to accomplish true self-control, it is through our dependence on the Holy Spirit. In Titus 1:7-8, self-control was an important virtue for leadership in the church. Proverbs 25:28 says, "Like a city that is broken into and without walls" is a person who lacks self-control."

The fruit of the Spirit are the characteristics of God, lived out through Jesus and available to us through the Holy Spirit. Galatians 5:23 says that regarding the fruit of the Spirit, "against such things there is no law," which means there is no law against the characteristics of the fruit of the Spirit because they are all good qualities that are not against the law. Could you imagine if everyone in the world was living out the fruit of the spirit? What a different world it would be to live in!

---

[126] Hebrews 10:23, I Corinthians 10:13, II Thessalonians 3:3, I John 1:9, I Peter 4:19
[127] John 8:3-11
[128] I Peter 3:15

Paul said in Philippians 1:6, "He who began a good work in you will perfect it till the day of Christ Jesus," which is true of all believers. We won't completely become like Jesus until we are in heaven. Until then, we can allow the Holy Spirit to continue to grow the Fruit of the Spirit in our lives, so we will be known by our fruit as we become more like Jesus.[129]

[129] Matthew 7:15-20

Just as there are benefits of displaying the fruit of the Spirit, there are also many benefits of eating fruit for our health.

Fruits are a good source of vitamins and minerals, and they are recognized for their role in preventing vitamin C and vitamin A deficiencies. People who incorporate fruit in their diet reduce the risk of chronic diseases such as type 2 diabetes, plus the potassium in the fruit can reduce the risk of heart disease and stroke. Potassium may also reduce the risk of developing kidney stones and help to decrease bone loss. Folate (folic acid) helps the body form red blood cells, and it helps prevent neural tube birth defects such as spina bifida. They also provide antioxidants that help repair the damage done by free radicals and so may protect against certain cancers. Fruits also have a positive impact on digestive health because of polyphenols found in fruit, which are antioxidants that have been shown to alter colon microecology and balance the proportion of healthy and harmful bacteria.

The most beneficial fruits to eat are from within a radius of 100 miles from your home. Apples are a good source of fiber and vitamin C. They also contain polyphenols, which may have numerous health benefits. I'm a big fan of an apple a day because it is relaxing to take your time to chew it, and it also helps my digestion. The cantaloupe is packed full of nutrients, including beta-carotene, vitamin C, folate, water, and fiber, all of which have many health benefits. Cherries are a good source of vitamin C, potassium, fiber, and antioxidants. They are also known to lower cholesterol and work well as an anti-inflammatory. Grapes are especially high in vitamins K and C, with high antioxidants to prevent chronic disease. Peaches are high in fiber, vitamins, and minerals, which also contain beneficial plant compounds, like antioxidants, that help to protect your body from aging and disease. Watermelon is a low-calorie fruit high in nutrients, especially carotenoids and vitamin C, and it helps hydrate. You should be cautious about eating precut melons in fruit trays from the grocery store because they can be contaminated with harmful bacteria. Also, fruits from other countries have been irradiated to destroy organisms that cause spoilage, extend shelf life, and control pests. Unfortunately, it also decreases the nutrients in fruit.

It is recommended that adults should have 2 cups of fruit a day and children should have around 1.5 cups. It is not a good combination of eating fruit with meat. The fruit will be held in the stomach longer because the stomach will take more time to break down the protein first. When the stomach digests the protein first, it can cause the fruit to ferment in the colon. Fermentation can cause smelly gas, bloating, heartburn, diarrhea, and burping. It is always best to eat your fruit separately or with vegetables. When you chew your food, it releases enzymes to help break the fruit down to get more nutrients plus fiber, and since you get more fiber, it minimizes the sugar in the fruit. When you process fruits in juices, sauces, and smoothies, you are breaking down the fiber, which maximizes sugar content. Bananas are high in sugar content until the sugars break down as they ripen, and that makes it a better choice to eat them ripe. All citrus fruit is harvested before ripening so they can be sent to other countries. The result of that is it makes the fruit more acidic for our body. So, it makes sense not to eat more oranges for Vitamin C to fight off colds because you need to make your body more alkaline with greens. Citrus fruit causes inflammation in the body, so if you have inflammatory problems like arthritis, they are not recommended. It is said that bananas are a good source of potassium for us to eat every day. However, that is not true either because you will get 40% more potassium in a potato than in a banana. If you want to compare fruit, then cantaloupe, watermelon, apricots, and cherries are all higher in potassium than bananas. We all love citrus fruit and other tropical fruits, but it is better to limit the amounts we eat.

Hopefully, these health tips will give you more insight into the benefits of fruit and the best choices. God has blessed us with such an amazing variety of fruit to enjoy!

ATTITUDES

"Have this attitude in yourselves which was also in Christ Jesus,"

Philippians 2:5-6

How do your attitudes affect your life? The Oxford Dictionary states that attitude is a feeling or way of thinking that affects a person's behavior. We are going to look at one of Jesus' messages from the Sermon on the Mount about the beatitudes.[130] The word beatitude comes from the Latin word "beatus," which means blessedness. Each beatitude is like a proverb with a statement of characteristics and blessings, which are packed full of meaning. When Jesus talks about the beatitudes, it depicts the attitude of those who will become citizens of His kingdom. These principles can be a guideline to check our attitudes before God!

"Blessed are the poor in spirit, for theirs is the kingdom of heaven" The phrase "poor in spirit" is not a reference to money but an attitude a person would have when they acknowledge they are incapable in their own strength to be good enough to draw near to God. A person acknowledges this when they confess their sins and accept Jesus as Savior because of what He accomplished through His death and resurrection. Also, as Christians, we should be humble to recognize that without Jesus, we can do nothing in our own strength spiritually.[131] The Kingdom of God, also called the Kingdom of Heaven in the Bible, is the spiritual realm over which God reigns as King in Heaven and Earth. When John the Baptist said, "Repent

---

[130] Matthew 5:3-11 NAS
[131] John 15:5

because the Kingdom of Heaven is at hand," it was because Jesus the King had come to visit earth.[132] The Kingdom of Heaven is made up of believers in Jesus, also known as the Bride or *Body of Christ*, who are a part of the Kingdom of Heaven on earth now, but will all be together in heaven. *"**Blessed** are those who mourn, because they will be comforted."* Those who mourn" speaks of those who express deep sorrow over sin and repent from their sins. This could be at the time of conversion, but also related to Christians when we give into sin, we would have the attitude of mourning as we repent for our sin. Then, God comforts us and gives us peace in forgiveness from the guilt of our sins.[133] *"**Blessed** are the gentle because they will inherit the earth."* The "gentle or meek" is having the attitude of being humble and patient while showing power for the benefit of others, as Jesus modeled. As Christians now, we take on this same attitude of gentleness, and as God's children, we will inherit the earth when heaven comes down to the new earth.[134] *"**Blessed** are those who hunger and thirst for righteousness, for they shall be satisfied."* The Jewish people were pursuing righteousness through justice and equality on earth, which could only be a temporal fix, and sadly, they missed the true purpose of Jesus. As Christians, we should have a hunger and thirst daily to know God better through his word so He can work through us to live a righteous life, and then we can truly be satisfied.[135] *"**Blessed** are the merciful, for they shall receive mercy."* We have received mercy from God, so in turn, we should be merciful to others. As we live out His mercy to others, He continues to show us His mercies each day.[136] *"**Blessed** are the pure in heart, for they shall see God."* We can appear to be pure outwardly, but the true test

---

[132] Matthew 3:2 NAS
[133] Psalm 32:5
[134] Revelation 21:1-4
[135] Matthew 6:33
[136] Lamentations 3:22-23

of purity is what is in the heart, which is sinful by nature. We can only be made pure of heart by the blood of Jesus so we can see God. I believe that if we stay fully centered on God that will keep us pure in heart.[137] *"Blessed are the peacemakers, for they shall be called sons of God."* In Romans 12:18 Paul says, "If possible, so far as it depends on you, be at peace with all men." God knows it is not possible to be at peace with everyone, but we are to try to do our part to keep peace with everyone we can. Our most important example is Jesus, who was the ultimate peacemaker, as He brought us to peace with God through His death on the cross. Therefore, we can be called Children of God[138] and become peacemakers to bring others peace with God by telling them about Jesus. *"Blessed are those who have been persecuted for the sake of righteousness."* True believers will stand for the righteousness of God's laws that go against the sin in the world, and when they do that, they will be persecuted. However, Jesus says not to be afraid of man who can kill our body, because they are unable to kill our soul, since our soul will continue to live on in heaven.[139] *"Blessed are you when men revile (criticize) you, persecute (victimize), and say all kinds of evil against you falsely, on the account of me."* Jesus said the world would hate people who accept Him because they hated Him first. Plus, God has taken us out of the world, so we are not of the world, and the world only loves its own.[140] We especially see that in North America in how Christians are being criticized more in our government, schools, and communities.

We are truly blessed as children of God as we look forward to the Kingdom of Heaven. Therefore, we can keep our attitudes in check

---

[137] Matthew 22:37
[138] I John 3:9-10
[139] Matthew 10:28
[140] John 15: 18-19

so we can truly be a salt and light to the world as a witness for God right now.[141]

---

[141] Matthew 5:13-16

THE PREFERENCE OF JUICING AND SMOOTHIES

If you read the B-Attitudes at face value, it sounds like they are talking about regular people. However, they have a much deeper meaning because these are attitudes, as believers in Christ, that we should have. Even though they sound negative, they have a much deeper meaning and a positive outcome. This is similar to juicing and smoothies because, quite often, people do not understand the difference and the benefits between the two. So, we are going to learn more about Juicing and Smoothies to compare the differences and the benefits of using them.

When you do juicing, you use a juicer machine to extract the juice from the fruit and vegetables. When the juice is being extracted, you lose some of the water and nutrients in the pulp that are left behind. The pulp is an important insoluble fiber that keeps your digestive tract healthy and slows down the absorption of sugar. My daughter uses the pulp to put in her muffins, so she does not waste all the good fiber. Greens are important in juicing because we need more greens to balance the pH in the body because you get more sugar content when there is no fiber. I am not a fan of doing my own juicing because of all the preparation it takes to get only a small amount of juice and all the cleanup of the juicer attachments. Juicing involves certain blends of vegetables and fruits that are medicinal for the body. I prefer to buy mine prepared from the health food store, in glass bottles, or from the freezer case. My favorite is beet, carrot, and apple blend that is good for the liver and helps my digestion. One of the main benefits of juicing is it helps rest the digestive tract from digesting fibers if you are having digestive problems.

You use a blender to make a smoothie, which pulverizes the whole produce, and there is no pulp left over. With smoothies, you get the important fiber that balances sugars, but you still might lose some nutrients in the fiber that get absorbed in the digestive tract. It is also good to add greens to your smoothie since too many fruits add a higher sugar intake. I add protein powder to my smoothies to make it a meal replacement. Vegetarian protein is best for my digestion, but whatever protein powder you get, read the ingredients to make sure it is pure ingredients without fillers. You can also find recipes that add avocado or other sources of protein. Try to stay away from milk and yogurt in your smoothie because they cause more inflammation in the body. You can use milk alternatives like almond or coconut milk. I substitute milk with coconut water, which is a great source of electrolytes. The main benefit of smoothies are they are a quick and easy way to get a nutritious meal or snack in a matter of minutes.

Make sure you always wash the produce with a fruit and veggie wash to get rid of parasites and other residue. When using bananas, choose the ripe ones to avoid consuming a higher amount of sugar. The best fruit choices are berries because they are high in antioxidants, plus kale and spinach for dark greens. The best source is organic fruits and vegetables because tests have proven they obtain the highest levels of nutrients. It is important to know that Strawberries and apples are grown with a higher number of chemical pesticides compared to other fruits. That is another reason it is important to use organic. It is best to get fresh fruits and vegetables, and you can always freeze them as needed. When I had my store, we had a smoothie bar, and we would have all the fruit and veggies prepared in portions to put in containers and freeze. This made it so much easier to make a smoothie quickly. Be cautious when buying frozen fruits, try reading the labels to see the location where they have been processed. This is because some fruits and vegetables are sent to China for processing, which can cause them to build up bacteria. A friend of mine bought a frozen bag of fruit from a big box store, and they had a call back on the bag of fruit, plus they gave the people an option for a free hepatitis shot.

Whole foods are especially important for healthy eating. When we chew our food, such as fruits, vegetables, nuts, seeds, sprouts, plus all other whole foods, we chew them to break them down in order to swallow them. In this process of chewing, the food gets covered with saliva, which contains an enzyme called Ptyalin. This enzyme helps to digest carbohydrates and begins the process of digestion in the mouth. When chewing food, you burn calories that help give the body energy, which keeps the body active and moving. When chewing fruits, it breaks down the sugars, but if you process the fruits in any way, they contain a much higher sugar count.

I have concluded that Juicing and Smoothies both have good benefits, but include dark greens that will give you extra enzymes for digestion. My suggestion would be to use them as a supplement only, since we need to eat whole food for better health and digestion.

WORDS

"Giving thanks and speaking bad words come from the same mouth. My Christian brothers, this is not right!"

James 3:10 NLV

Have you ever said something you wish you could take back? In this study, we are going to look at words and how they impact our lives. It says in Proverbs 18:21, "Death and life are in the power of the tongue," which means words can wound or heal the spirit of a person. We are going to compare the results of bad words, good words, and God's words in our lives.

When I was in elementary school, if someone would say something mean, we would say, "Sticks and stones can break my bones, but words can never hurt me." That was a defense to protect our self from the harsh words, but they did hurt and sometimes were hard to forget. Recently, my 13-year-old grandson told me that a group of boys would always say mean things to him. I tried to console him by jokingly telling him what we would say when I was a child. He said to me Grandma, that is definitely not true, which brought tears to my eyes. Then I said, so true because words can hurt you much deeper. We often say children can be cruel with their words, but adults can be cruel with their words too. Words seem like such a small thing, but they can have so much power over us. In James 3:2-8, he compares the power of our small tongue, which enables us to say words, is like a small bit in a horse's mouth and a small rudder on a large ship. This implies small things can have such power over

118

something bigger than itself and how that relates to the power and control of the tongue. James then goes on to imply how words can completely destroy someone and compares it to how a small spark can destroy a complete forest. We can even say something simple to our spouse or child, like they are annoying, instead of saying what they are doing is annoying. Even though it seems harmless, it could make them believe that is what you always think about them, which could lead them to start acting it out more. It seems like bad words are easier to say, especially when we are mad or aggravated about something. Before we speak, consider how words go deep and can kill the spirit of a person like it says in Proverbs 12:18, "There is one who speaks rashly like the thrust of a sword." It is very difficult to take back words once they have been spoken. Even Jesus warns us about our words in Matthew 12:36 when He says, "I tell you, on the day of judgment people will give account for every careless word they speak." Hopefully, these words from Jesus will encourage us to think before we speak. If this is something you struggle with, pray that God will help you think before you speak and the Holy Spirit will give you words as it tells us in Ephesians 4:29, "Let no harmful word come out of your mouth, but only what is beneficial for building others up according to the need, so that it gives grace to those who hear it."

Think about when you have felt really down because of a bad day, and someone has said a good word to you, and how that lifts your spirit.[142] In Proverbs it tells us there are many benefits to good words because they bring healing, turn away anger, and are like honey to the soul. It reminds me of the golden rule of Jesus' words in Matthew 7:12, which says, "Do unto others as you would wish

---

[142] Proverbs 12:18, Proverbs 15:1, Proverbs 16:24

them to do to you." Just talk to someone in a way you would like them to talk to you, with good encouraging words. If we are speaking good words, it fulfills our desire to have our words be acceptable in God's sight.[143]

God's words are so powerful He spoke creation into existence.[144] Matthew 24:35 tells us that when everything else passes away, His word will not pass away. In Luke 18:19, Jesus said, "no one is good except God," so that would mean His words are good, too. When someone calls us good, we are not consistently good like God because His nature never changes, unlike people because of our sinful nature. God's word is powerful in our life as it says in Hebrews, "The word of God is sharper than any two-edged sword "which discern the thoughts and intentions of our heart."[145] In Psalm 119:105 it says, "God's word is a lamp to my feet and light to my path.," and that is why it is important to read His word every day. It will guide you on the path through life and keep you from stumbling away from Him. It is such a wonderful thing to feel loved, but God's love is so much more than human love! God's word says because of "His great mercy we are born again into a living hope to an imperishable inheritance through the resurrection of Jesus from the dead." God uses words such as we are His children, nothing can separate us from His love, and His love never fails us.[146] Paul tries to explain God's Love for us in Ephesians 3:18-19 when he says "and to know the love of Christ which surpasses knowledge" to help us fully understand the depth of His love for us.

---

[143] Psalm 19:14
[144] Genesis chapter 1
[145] Hebrews 4:12 NAS
[146] 1 John 3:1, Romans 8:38-39, 1 Chronicles 16:34

It is clear that bad words are never helpful to speak or receive, good words have a positive effect on those who speak or receive them, and of course, God's words always have a purpose, which result for good.

Our words should reflect the good that God has placed in our hearts now we know Jesus.

THE POSITIVE AND NEGATIVE OF
SUNSCREEN

We want to choose our words wisely to do good and not harm. We also need to choose our sunscreen wisely to protect our skin and not do more harm than good in the process. With sunscreen, we need to check the labels to see if there are harmful chemicals in the ingredients and choose the most natural with the best ingredients.

We are told we should wear sunscreen to protect our skin from cancer. We are going to look at the real truth of this because there are negative effects of wearing sunscreen. Sunscreens use one or more chemicals which include Oxybenzone, Avobenzone, Octisalate, Octocrylene, Homosalate, and Octinorate. Sunscreens with chemicals in them commonly include ingredients that act as "penetration enhancers," which help the products to adhere to the skin. A spray sunscreen can be even more harmful because you are breathing in tiny particles of the chemicals. Many of the chemicals in sunscreen can be absorbed into the body and have been found in blood, breast milk, and urine samples. Most brands of sunscreen have toxic chemicals such as: *Oxybenzone* which is linked to hormone disruption and cell damage that leads to skin cancer. *Retinyl palmitate* which has now been proven to be carcinogenic. *Butyl methoxydibenzoylmethane* releases free radicals into the body. *Benzophenone 2 (BP 2)* decreases the function of the thyroid, causing hypothyroidism (underactive).

It makes sense to search out natural sunscreen that uses minerals like Zinc, Titanium, or Micah, because they are natural minerals that create a physical barrier to protect the skin from the sun. In your search, also look for one that contains antioxidants such as

Vitamin C and E, which are crucial to defending against skin inflammation. However, read the labels well because just because they say they are natural and have a few natural ingredients, they might also have some harmful chemicals added. You can Google BWG (Environmental Working Group) to check out the safest sunscreens to use. However, sunscreen is not enough because you need to enhance your sun protection from within your body, too. Vitamin C is very important to take in the summer, too, because it is an important supplement to protect your skin. Plus, Vitamin E, green supplements, omega 3, and Aloe Vera Juice all help to protect the skin.

There are definitely benefits of the sun, too, but since there is such fear of the sun, people wear sunscreen all the time, which can make people Vitamin D deficient. Sunscreens stop the sun's ultraviolet rays from creating Vitamin D in the body, which is essential for many functions such as: *bone health, prevents cancer, supports the immune system, protects against dementia, good for losing extra fat, essential for decreasing asthma, strengthens teeth, and good for overall health.*

The retina is the only outside nerve that has direct contact with the brain, so it is the best way to get the sun's rays directly to the brain. When the sun's rays enter the brain via the optic nerve, it stimulates the pituitary gland to secrete HGH (human growth hormones). This significantly boosts the entire immune system, as well as being good for eye health. The most harmful rays are between 10:00 am – 2:00 pm. So before 10:00 am and after 2:00 pm it is safe to go without sunscreen and sunglasses because it will benefit the whole body.

Of course, if you are going to be out all day, especially around the water, you will want to wear good sunglasses to prevent sun glare on your eyes. When you buy quality sunglasses, look for Polarized, darker lenses, mirror coated, and wrap around for the best protection for your eyes.

BUILDING UP

"Therefore encourage one another, and build up one another, just as you also are doing."

I Thessalonians 5:11

When Jesus' death was near, He went with a heavy heart to his father and prayed for the born-again Christians to become one, just as He is with His Father.[147] Our top priority should be our unity since it was a burden on the heart of Jesus to pray for us to be one with each other. We can help to accomplish unity through building up each other. Let's look at verses in the Bible that encourage unity and why it is important.

Some people think it is enough just watching church from home, but if you do not have that personal contact with other believers, how can you build relationships that will build a bond of unity?[148] Building up starts with making sure we get together with each other for fellowship in church, bible studies, and prayer groups. As we are together, we get to know each other better to "stimulate one another to love and do good deeds."[149] We also need a humble attitude of thinking that everyone is more important than us to avoid conflict as we have fellowship with other believers.[150] Church splits could be avoided if we truly practiced humility in the church. We all have different personalities, which causes us to have different opinions, but we should not allow that to divide us because

---

147 John 17:20-26
148 Colossians 3:14-16
149 Hebrews 10:24-25 NAS
150 Philippians 2:3-4

of our bond of unity with Jesus.[151] Jesus said, "A new commandment I give you, that you love one another, even as I have loved you", and by this, all men would know that we are His disciples.[152] As a church congregation of people in a building, do people know us because of our love for each other?

A good practical example of building each other up is in the book of Nehemiah. As you read it, you will realize there was much more happening than just building a wall around Jerusalem. It was because of the Jewish people's disobedience to God that the Babylonians seized Jerusalem, burned the gates, tore the walls down, and took the people captive for 70 years. Nehemiah missed his homeland of Jerusalem and knew the importance of getting the wall back up around the city for protection and to establish them as a Jewish nation again. Nehemiah remembered God's promise to the Jewish people that if they returned to Him, asked for forgiveness, and kept His commandments, then He would restore them. Nehemiah had been praying God would put on the heart of the new king the desire to allow his people to build the wall.[153] Since Nehemiah was the king's cupbearer, he was able to talk with the king to let him know his need to build the wall. Then God answered Nehemiah's prayer request, and the king agreed to let them go build a wall around Jerusalem.[154] Nehemiah's people all had a common bond of the desire to get their wall rebuilt. Then Nehemiah arranged all the plans for the wall by dividing it into sections to enable them all to have a part in building it by working together. They were each given responsibilities for building, plus they had to be prepared to protect each other from evil men who were trying to keep them from

---

[151] Romans 14:19
[152] John 13:34-35 NAS
[153] Nehemiah 1:1-11
[154] Nehemiah 2:1-8

completing the wall.[155] After the wall was finished, the priest read the Book of the Law. As they listened, they became convicted of their sin of disobedience and repented to become renewed. Afterward, they celebrated the unity they now had with God and each other. This is such a great example of Christians having a common goal, each to use their own giftings to work together to serve, protect each other, and to be receptive to God's word.[156]

God has given each one of us amazing gifts to use that can complement each other's work as we work together for Him. Our obedience to God and our common bond of unity in Jesus will make it possible for us to build each other up, which will develop unity with our Christian brothers and sisters. Through this, we will become one, which can be the answer to Jesus's prayer. When we have this mindset, it will help us to think before we tear each other down.

We can accomplish so much more by building each other up, and then we can truly work together as one for God's Glory!

---

[155]Nehemiah 4:6-9
[156] Romans 12:4-5

MUSCLES TO BUILD UP

It is important to build each other up in our Christian faith to keep unity in the body of Christ. It is also important to keep our muscles built up to support our human body. When we think of keeping our muscles built up, it makes us think of bodybuilders. However, most body-builders who work on their muscles are more interested in appearance than healthy muscles. We are going to look at a brief explanation of muscles and the important role they have in supporting our body. Hopefully, this information will allow you to see the importance of your muscles and how to keep them healthy and function the way that God intended.

The muscular system is responsible for movement, posture, and internal functions of the human body. Attached to the bones of the skeletal system are about 700 named muscles that make up about 40% of total body weight. Each of these muscles is a discrete organ constructed of skeletal muscle tissue, blood vessels, tendons, and nerves. Muscle tissue is also found inside of the heart, digestive organs, and blood vessels. In these organs, muscles serve to move substances throughout the body. Most skeletal muscles are attached with two bones through tendons. Tendons are tough bands of dense, regular connective tissue whose strong collagen fibers rigidly attach the muscles to the bones. Tendons are under extreme stress when muscles pull on them, so they are strong and are woven into the coverings of both muscles and bones. Muscles move by shortening their length, pulling on tendons, and moving bones closer to each other. One of the bones is pulled towards the other bone, which remains stationary. The belly of the muscle is the fleshy part of the muscle in between the tendons that cause the actual contraction.

Many people are confused as to how muscles work. In fact, muscles can only pull or contract and not push. Every day, muscles work in pairs so that a person can bend to pick things up and do other movements. In these types of movement, one muscle inside the body lengthens, and the other shortens. The one that shortens is the one that contracts. This is a brief description of muscles because, like everything God has created, muscles are also very intricate, and there is so much more that can be explained about them. Just like everything God has created in the body, the muscles are dependent on other parts of the body to work.

Healthy muscles let you move freely and keep your body strong. They help you to enjoy playing sports, dancing, walking, swimming, and other fun activities. Then, they also help you do those other not-so-fun things that you have to do, like making the bed, vacuuming the floor, or mowing the lawn. Strong muscles also help to keep your joints in decent shape. For example, if the muscles around your knees get weak, you may be more likely to injure the knees. Strong muscles also help you keep your balance, so you are less likely to slip or fall. The activities that make your skeletal muscles strong will also help to keep your heart muscle strong! So, it is important to stay active even if you can only do stretches and gentle impact exercises every week.

Eating healthy food and taking supplements can also help to keep muscles strong, which will help prevent and can correct problems with your muscles. Muscles need high-protein food in your diet, such as meat, beans, eggs, Greek yogurt, and cottage cheese, and you can supplement it with whey powder protein. Vegetarians plus people who are lactose intolerant can find high protein in Spirulina, seeds, nuts, peanut butter, nutritional yeast, beans, non-GMO tofu, dark green vegetables, and vegetarian or vegan protein powder.

Muscles also need 40-60% carbohydrates, which include naturally occurring sugars, starch, and cellulose, which would be your vegetables and fruit. They contain hydrogen and oxygen in the same ratio as water (2:1) and typically can break down to release energy in the body. Although carbohydrates are important, eating the wrong types of carbs can be detrimental to your health. Eating candy is a high glycemic sugar that certainly will not do anything to help improve your health overall. Processed foods with added sugars are poor sources of quality carbohydrates in your diet. It is important to limit most of your carbohydrate intake to nutrient-dense foods. Nutrient-dense, high-carb foods include fruits, vegetables, greens, beets, cauliflower, yams, chick peas, brown rice, quinoa, lentils and whole grains .

It is impossible to get all the nutrients from our foods because of we do not eat perfect. So, you can also take a good food-based multivitamin that will help supplement that extra bit of nutrients that you might need. There are also special nutrients that the muscles need to be healthy, which you can take, especially if you are struggling with muscle-related conditions. Supplements for keeping the muscles healthy are Collagen, Magnesium, Amino Acids, Fish Oil, B-complex, Vitamin B1, Vitamin D, Vitamin C, and Vitamin E.

HOW IS YOUR VISION

"For we live by faith, not by sight-"

II Corinthians 5:7

I started using magnifying glasses to read smaller print, which seems to happen to most of us as we age. However, there became more of a need to wear glasses when I began to write. Then, it seemed a wise decision to make an appointment with the Optometrist. At the appointment, the optometrist found out that not only were my eyes becoming farsighted, but one eye was weaker than the other. The best solution was to purchase reading glasses to correct the right amount of vision needed for each eye. It seems funny that I have always found the description of the condition for eyesight confusing, but I do understand it now. Although, in my mind, it makes sense to be the opposite, that if you cannot see things near, you would be nearsighted, and when you cannot see things far away, you would be farsighted. Let's consider how our spiritual *vision* should be and what our *focus* should look like.

Most of the time, we only *look* at the immediate everyday needs as if we can take care of them. We think they are not important enough to ask God for help because we can *see* ways to solve things by ourselves. We might not even *see* the things God is doing for us because we *see* the answer to our circumstances just worked out. In our daily walk of faith, we should be *looking* for results from God in the small everyday things that work out for the best in our lives, too. Sometimes, even when the big things come into our lives, we see them as impossible to change by ourselves or even trust God to change. Jesus tells us in Matthew 17:20 that if we have "faith as small as a mustard seed, we can move a mountain." That means when we have even the smallest of faith, we can trust God to move those big things that are in our *view*, blocking our goals. Sometimes, we forget Luke 1:37, which tells us that "nothing is impossible for God," even when it seems too huge to *see* our way around it. We also like to *look* to the future and worry about how things will work together. Jesus tells us to *seek* Him first and not *focus* on the future because "each day has enough trouble of its own."[157]

We can keep our *vision focused* when we read the Bible each day to learn more about God, memorize the word to keep us from sin, use the word as a light so we can *see* our direction, and "fix our *eyes* on Jesus, the author, and perfector of our faith."[158] God has given us so many promises that can keep our *focus* on the assurance of our relationship with Him, such as we are loved as children, nothing can separate us from His love, He is in control of our circumstances, and He never changes.[159] Spiritual *vision* also improves our *sight* on how we *see* people who don't know Jesus, as *blind* and lost, searching for something to fill the empty space that only God can.[160] The disciples were given the great commission of reaching out to others and God has given each of us our own mission field where we live.[161] Jesus said that we are "the light of the world," so we can reflect Jesus for people to *see* that He is the only way to God.[162] I know it is not always easy to share our faith, but we can let our light shine so Jesus can be *seen* from our actions, which can speak louder than words until you need the words.

---

[157] Matthew 6:33-34 NAS
[158] II Timothy 3:16, Psalms 119:11, Psalm 119:105, Hebrews 12:2 NAS
[159] I John 3:1, Romans 8:38-39, John 10:27-29, Romans 8:28, Hebrews 13:8
[160] Ecclesiastes 3:11
[161] Matthew 28:19-20
[162] Matthew 5:14-16 NAS

I admire Peter because he was enthusiastic as he served Jesus, even though he had some failures along the way. Jesus knew Peter's strong love and his commitment to Him, so maybe that was the reason Peter was in Jesus' inner circle along with John and James. He included them in special events such as Jesus appearing in His glorious splendor.[163] Peter revealed who Jesus truly was through divine intervention, and then Jesus went on to tell Peter he would be used to build the church, which is the Body of Christ that no one can destroy.[164] Peter later went on to write the first Gospel that was scribed by Mark. Peter was also an advocate for the other apostles and the first person that God revealed that the Gentiles would be saved also.[165] Peter's *focus* on Jesus gave him the *vision* to build the kingdom of God for 30 years as he traveled to set up churches, preach, and heal. During those years, he was persecuted, imprisoned, and eventually died for his faith.

In Hebrews 11:1, it says, "Faith is the assurance of things hoped for, the convictions of things not *seen*." In Hebrews 11:6, it says, "Without Faith, it is impossible to please God." We find our faith gives us hope when our *eyes* are fixed on Jesus, surrendering our will to our Heavenly Father, and trusting His promises.

Our true *vision* is our faith in God, not our *sight* of temporary things in the world that will not last. This helps us to *focus* on what will last for eternity.

---

[163] Matthew 17:1-9
[164] Matthew 16:13-18
[165] Acts 4:5-22,5:1-10, Chapter 10: - Chapter11:18

EYE HEALTH

God has wonderfully created our eyes to give us vision to experience not only sight but to enjoy His beautiful creation in color.

Like all the parts of the body that God has created, the eyes are no exception of being intricately made. All the various parts of the eyes work together to help us see. First, light passes through the **cornea, which is** the clear front layer of the eye. The cornea is shaped like a dome and bends light to help the eye focus. Some of this light enters the eye through an opening called the **pupil**. The colored part of the eye is the **iris,** which controls how much light the pupil lets in. Then, the light passes through the **lens**, which is the clear inner part of the eye. The lens works together with the cornea to focus light correctly on the retina. When light hits the **retina, which** is a light-sensitive layer of tissue at the back of the eye, special cells called photoreceptors turn the light into electrical signals. These electrical signals travel from the retina through the **optic nerve** to the brain. Then, the brain turns the signals into the images we see. This is a basic description of how the eyes work but there is so much more involved in the working of the eye.

It is amazing to think that the eyes make 15 to 30 gallons of tears each year for the eyes to work correctly. Tears serve many purposes, and the eyes produce them all the time. Tears are essential to help us to see clearly and maintain the health of our eyes plus they can also help communicate our emotions. The body makes three types of tears, which are Basal tears that are in our eyes all the time to lubricate, nourish and protect the cornea. Reflex tears are formed when your eyes need to wash away harmful irritants, such as smoke, foreign objects, or onion fumes. The eyes release these in larger amounts than basal tears, and they may contain more antibodies to help fight bacteria. Emotional tears are produced in response to joy, sadness, fear, and other emotional states. The emotional tears contain additional hormones and proteins not found in the other tears. This is just the basic information on tears to help you see how God has made everything for a purpose.

Everyone knows how important our eyesight is to us. So, it makes sense that we want to protect our eyes and take care of them. Natural light is a full spectrum light, which is light that includes a balance of wavelengths from colors of the visible spectrum including ultraviolet and infrared. This form of natural light is beneficial to our health when it contacts the skin, and the eyes because it plays a vital role in the body chemistry for our health. It provides Vitamin D which is not only important to absorb through our skin but also our eyes. However, we block those rays from our eyes with UV light-blocking sunglasses. There is a role for sunglasses, but UV light is safe for our eyes if we are outside before 10 am and after 2 pm. So, it is helpful for the eyes to get in the sun for 20-60 minutes a day without wearing glasses if we want to absorb more vitamins for our eyes. Also, it is healthier for your eyes to have full spectrum lighting indoors rather than cool-white lighting.

If you cannot get outside enough, you should supplement with extra emulsified vitamin D drops. Also, if you live in Canada or the north, you will never get the amount of sun you need to get all the vitamin D your body requires. If you have S.A.D. (Seasonal Affective Disorder), it means that you also need extra vitamin D. When Vitamin D is emulsified, the fats have been broken down so you can absorb it better, and it will not build up toxins in the fat cells if you

137

take higher doses. You can also take supplements for eye strength like Lutein, Zinc, B Complex, Vitamin C, and Omega Oils high in DHA. There are also single supplements that you can take specifically for the eyes that have a lot of these ingredients in them, but I would suggest still taking extra Vitamin C and DHA too.

DECISIONS AND DIRECTION

"Trust in the Lord with all your heart, and do not lean on your own understanding. In all your ways acknowledge Him, and He will make your path straight."

Proverbs 3:5-6

Seems like there are so many decisions to make in life. Some are easy decisions that are not life changing. These are usually decisions we need to make right away, such as what we want in our coffee, what we will wear, and choosing a restaurant. Then there are life changing decisions that take more time to decide, which are such things as deciding on a university, choosing a spouse, and making major financial purchases. We are going to look at making decisions and finding direction from the perspective of the Bible.

In the Bible it talks about the word of God being our food and even Jesus said He is the bread of life.[166] How can we live a healthy life for God if we are not consuming His word each day as our spiritual food? If we do not eat food our body suffers from malnutrition. This causes poor health, which results in a body that cannot function properly for a normal life. This is the same idea as our spiritual food. If we do not read the Bible each day, we suffer from spiritual malnutrition that causes us to become unhealthy in our spiritual growth, and our close relationship with God suffers. As you stay close to God in your relationship each day, He will give you the "desires of your heart" that will help you to know His will.[167] The

---

[166] John 6:35
[167] Psalm 37:4-5 NAS

Bible is important to give us direction to lead and guide us on our way through life, as it says in Psalms 119:105, "Thy Word is a lamp to my feet and a light unto my path."

We can become anxious when making decisions because of the uncertainty of making the right choice. As Christians when we read our Bible, it gives us guidelines for making decisions, such as seeking God first to provide, to "be anxious for nothing", but to take everything to God in prayer.[168] As you center your life around God, you can trust Him to work it all together to accomplish what is best for you, which is not always what we think is best.[169] There are also situations where God might be calling you to make an immediate decision, like helping a homeless person you see living on the street or giving money to a visiting missionary. We need to be sensitive to the Holy Spirit, prompting us to make the decision God wants us to make.[170] The Bible does not give you exact answers like what university to attend or who you should marry. Although, there is the promise that when we need wisdom, just ask God, and He will give it to us.[171] God will not make our decisions for us because that is our responsibility. However, we need to keep in mind that when deciding what to do, that our decision should never contradict God's word.

When God impressed on my heart to write a devotional book, there were decisions for me to make. Since teaching Bible studies for many years, I became interested because it would be writing things God has taught me through the years in His word. However, I had never written a book, so it was overwhelming to think about writing devotions to cover a year. As I began to write the devotional, it

---

[168] Matthew 6:33, Philippians 4:6 NAS
[169] Romans 8:28
[170] John 16:13-14, I Corinthians 2:12-13
[171] James 1:5

became evident that it was becoming more than a devotional since my passion has always been teaching Bible studies. My husband suggested adding some of my healthy recipes, plus the thought came to me to use my knowledge from training in natural health by adding health tips. Then all the ideas began to flow together and as God inspired me, I would write thoughts down in a notebook. Writing for me was not easy because it took me longer than I thought, since I had to do a lot of rewrites. However, it was exciting to see how God's hand was at work in everything to put all the thoughts together in this book, and the benefit for me was growing in more knowledge about God that brought me nearer to Him.

God can speak to us through the Holy Spirit in prayer, reading the Bible, when talking to trusted mentors or friends, different circumstances that happen in our life, and a lot of times for me, even when I'm working around the house. God usually speaks to us in a still, small voice, like He did for me, and then He placed the desire in my heart.[172] The Christian life is a daily spiritual walk and not a marathon, as we build our faith.[173] As you stay in God's word and pray about your decision, you need to keep walking forward to see what doors will open or close as "the Lord directs your steps".[174]

If you can establish from the beginning of the decision, you are putting your trust in God, you can be reassured that He will give you direction, as it tells us in our theme verse, Proverbs 3:5-6.

---

[172] I Kings 19:11-13
[173] II Corinthians 5:7, Galatians 5:25
[174] Proverbs 16:9 NAS

RESULTS OF READING

Just as there are many benefits of reading the Bible there are also other kinds of benefits when you read a book. I'm not an avid reader but do enjoy reading the things I'm passionate about. Such as the Bible every day, books on Biblical topics, plus books and articles on health. My mother was not a reader and never encouraged me to read, so most of my reading was in school. I always read to my children a story at nap time and a devotional at bedtime. When my youngest daughter started kindergarten, she asked the teacher why she was reading a book because it wasn't time for a nap. So, that was a little embarrassing when the teacher told me that!

Reading is not only good for your mental health but for your physical health too! First, of course, is *mental stimulation*, which studies have shown that staying mentally stimulated can slow the progress or even the prevention of Alzheimer's and Dementia because it keeps your brain active. It also helps *stress reduction* because no matter how much stress you have in your life, it slips away when you lose yourself in a remarkable story, which can also be helpful for *blood pressure*. Doctors have found it gives you a better night's *sleep* if you read before going to bed. It helps to ease *depression* because when you are reading fiction, it can allow you to temporarily escape your own world. It seems those that read regularly might *live longer*.

Along with all these benefits of reading, it is also beneficial to read up on natural health to help with prevention of health problems. Prevention is always the best medicine, without side effects. It always works best to choose to be responsible for the care of your own health. As I always say, God has given us an amazing body that can heal itself if we give the body the nutrients it is lacking.

Prevention is to make sure you are eating healthy and taking vitamins and supplements you need to supply the needs of your body. It is difficult for most people to eat perfectly, so it is good to take a *Multivitamin*, a *Green* supplement to balance pH, and *Fish Oil*, which will give you more good fats for the brain and help the joints. If you have other health concerns, you can read up on the best natural remedies to heal or relieve them. You can also go to your local Health Food Store for recommendations of which are the best products to take for your health needs or concerns and read up on what you think is the best choice for you.

Reading up on health and nutrition will enable you to stay healthy so you can read longer!

KEEP IN THE MOMENT

"And hope does not disappoint, because the love of God has been poured out within our hearts through the Holy Spirit who was given to us."

Romans 5:5

When you think about it, everyone has been disappointed at various times in their life. In the Oxford dictionary, the definition of disappointment is sadness or displeasure caused by the nonfulfillment of one's hopes or expectations. My experience with disappointment has made me think about it as being one of the most discouraging emotions. It is a form of delayed expectation, failed plans, abandoned dreams, and sometimes destroyed hope in someone or something. However, we are going to look at how God can give us hope that rises during disappointment when we keep in the moment, so we do not miss what God has for us.

If we are always thinking about past disappointments or future hopes, we cannot keep in the moment to appreciate what God has for us now. In John 16:33, Jesus tells us, "in this world we will have troubles" and disappointment can be a result of that. What we are really saying if we stay in disappointment is that we are not happy with what God has allowed in our lives. After any disappointment, ask yourself, is my hope in my plan or "the Lord who directs my steps."[175] There is nothing wrong with making plans, but it is best to think or say, "If the Lord wills, we shall live and do this or that,"

---

[175] Proverbs 16:9 NAS

to acknowledge God has the final say in our plans.[176] As we process our disappointment, it is good to take it to God in prayer and thank Him. This shows our obedience, and it recognizes He is in control of our plans.[177] God wants us to trust Him completely and not to depend on our own understanding but to recognize Him in all aspects of our lives so He can make our "paths straight."[178]

Another aspect to think about is what does God want to teach me through this disappointment. Let's consider what God was teaching Jacob with some disappointments he dealt with in his life.[179] Jacob had to leave his home because he deceived his brother Esau out of his inheritance. His mother sent him to live with her brother Laban in his homeland, so Esau would not harm him. Jacob falls in love with Laban's younger daughter, Rachael, and Laban tells Jacob he will have to work for him seven years before he can marry Rachael. Then, after seven years Laban explained that the oldest daughter must marry first. Again, Laban told Jacob he would have to work another seven years to marry Rachael. Finally, after seven more years, Laban permitted Jacob to marry Rachael, his true love. Through the years, Leah had many children, but it became a disappointment to Jacob when Rachel could not have children. Years later, God remembered Rachael, and she bore a son that they named Joseph. After Rachael had a son, Jacob asked Laban if he could go back to his homeland with his wives and children. Laban had prospered while Jacob was with him and was not anxious for Jacob to go. However, Jacob devised a plan to divide up the livestock so he could go, but Laban became very unfriendly with him. Then God told Jacob to get his family packed up and leave Laban's

---

[176] James 4:13-15 NAS
[177] I Thessalonians 5:18
[178] Proverbs 3:5-6 NAS
[179] Genesis chapter 29-33

homeland for his own. In Jacob's travels back he heard his brother Esau was coming, then he became afraid of what his brother would do to him. As Jacob met his brother Esau on the road home, they were able to make things right with each other. However, Jacob told his brother he would meet up with him later, but he lied because he still didn't trust Esau. Then Jacob traveled in another direction instead of keeping his word and trusting God. On the trip, Rachael had a son they named Benjamin, but she died in childbirth, and Jacob was heartbroken. Jacob lived up to his name, which means deceiver, and it seems in Jacob's case, God was using his disappointments through Laban to teach him what the consequence of deception feels like. Hopefully, we will be sensitive to the Holy Spirit and understand what God is teaching us in each disappointment.

We can trust God's promises in the Bible because "the Word is God," and He is the "same yesterday, today, and forever," which means the promises in the Bible never change.[180] Jesus said in Mark 10:18, "no one is good except God," which means He is holy, pure, and righteous, and that means only the good in your life comes from God. The world can cause various problems and disappointments, but God promises in II Corinthians 12:9 that His grace is sufficient to help us in our weakness. Take a moment in your disappointment to thank God because He is Sovereign to shield us from hurt, harm, and danger. Although, sometimes He is teaching us something to grow our faith and even use our trials to help comfort others as we have been comforted, as it tells us in II Corinthians 1:4. Paul explains in Romans 5:1-5, when we stand firm in our faith, the hardships develop perseverance, proven character and hope that does not disappoint because of the love we have in our hearts

---

[180] John 1:1, Hebrews 13:8 NAS

through the Holy Spirit. We not only have the promise He lives in our hearts, but we experience it through the work of the Holy Spirit in our lives every day!

Keep in the moment of disappointment, to know God can teach you something through it and trust God that He can use it for good. We know people and circumstances will always cause disappointment but our hope in God's promises will never disappoint us!

STEPS TO HELP PARKINSON'S DISEASE

Receiving the news of having Parkinson's disease can be very disappointing to a person. It is the uncertainty of knowing exactly how it will affect the future of your health and your abilities. Also, your future dreams may have to change.

In Parkinson's disease, certain nerve cells (neurons) in the brain gradually break down or die. Many of the symptoms are due to a loss of neurons that produce a chemical messenger in your brain called dopamine. When dopamine levels decrease, it causes abnormal brain activity, leading to impaired movement and other symptoms of the disease. The cause of Parkinson's is unknown, but they think certain factors appear to play a role, such as a certain gene variation, which appears to increase but with a small risk of the disease for each of these genetic markers. It may also be exposure to certain toxins or environmental factors that increase the risk of the disease later in life since people usually develop the disease around 60's.

Parkinson's disease signs and symptoms can be different for everyone. Early signs may be mild and go unnoticed. Symptoms often begin on one side of your body and usually remain worse on that side when symptoms begin to affect both sides. The signs and symptoms may include tremors in an arm, ridged muscles, impaired posture and balance, loss of control of movement, speech changes, and writing changes.

My father was diagnosed with Parkinson's in his mid-60's. He lived to 94 years old on medication and lived an active life with only minor shaking in his hands at times. In my 60's, I began to have tremors in my left hand but chose to control it naturally. I went to a Chelation Doctor and received extensive testing for heavy metals. My test results came back with considerable amounts of lead in my body, but I decided not to do chelation therapy because of the extensive cost and time it would take. So, I decided to do oral chelation by taking larger doses of minerals and therapy on my PEMF matt that was in my clinic. I believe the thing that was most helpful in removing the effects of the tremor in my arm was the PEMF matt.

The PEMF matt is a pulsating electromagnetic frequency based on the low pulsating frequencies from the earth, which balance and heal. The body has a lot of high frequencies (EMF) to deal with due to all the high frequencies in our homes and now even more so because of all cell phone towers, microwave towers, and many satellite transmissions. The PEMF matt uses lower frequencies that can remove a lot of the effect of the EMF on the body so it can heal. Every ailment, disease, and medical challenge can benefit from the PEMF matt. You can search the internet for more information and find clinics that offer this treatment in your area.

It is also important to eat nutritious whole foods and not a lot of processed foods. That would include all foods high in protein and fiber, such as green leafy vegetables, fruit, nuts, grains like quinoa and rice, as well as seeds like sunflower, sesame, and beans. Recommended supplements would be, Omega 3 with a higher amount of DHA (source small fish), Vitamin D, CoQ10, B-12 with folic acid, and B-Complex along with extra B-6. Also, a healthy gut is important, so keep the colon clean and provide extra probiotics. Since the lack of dopamine in the brain, the amino acid that help produce dopamine is Tyrosine. These are all useful sources to nourish the brain and the nervous system.

Hope these suggestions are helpful for you to prevent Parkinson's and if you already have it, they should help to minimize the effects.

PROBLEMS

"In the world you have tribulation, but take courage; I have overcome the world."

In the verse John 16:32-33, Jesus is preparing the disciples for when He departs from earth, by forewarning them about the problems to come. Although Jesus comforts them with a promise that only He can give them peace for the problems to come. At that time, the disciples didn't fully understand when Jesus gave them this promise because He would overcome the world by the results of His death on the cross. We all would like to go through our lives without any problems, but that would be like having sunshine every day for our gardens without rain. Just like your garden couldn't grow, we could not grow in our faith without problems in our lives. Since we know our lives will have problems, let's look at them as opportunities for God to use in our lives for good.

First, we will look at some problems other people in the Bible had in their lives. In the Old Testament King David had a lot of problems in his life.[181] David was the youngest of 7 brothers, and tradition was that the youngest son would take over from his older brother, around 9 years old, to become the shepherd for the household. The problem with this job was after the Spring he would have to travel away from his home to find pastures with grass to feed his sheep. Then, he would have to deal with weather conditions and always be

---

[181] I Samuel chapter 16-31

on guard to keep his sheep safe from bears and lions. David was only 15 when he was anointed by Samuel to be the next king, and the Holy Spirit left Saul. Then King Saul had an evil spirit that would come over him, so he took David from being a shepherd to play the lyre to calm him. Saul liked David, then made him his armor-bearer and later allowed David to marry his daughter. As time went on Saul became so overwhelmed with jealousy of David that it became a problem, and in a fit of rage, Saul threw a spear at David as he played the lyre for him. After that event, Saul became determined to kill David, and David had to flee for his life. These are just a few of the problems David encountered before he was king, but he stayed strong in his trust in God. After David was king, he had problems caused by his sin of a series of bad choices. David's son Ammon raped his sister, and David did nothing about it, as if the problem would just go away.[182] That resulted with David's son Absalom killing his brother Ammon. Later, Absalom turned his anger on David to kill him, and David had to flee for his life.[183] Another bad choice that caused King David problems from sin was with Bathsheba. David should have been at battle but stayed home, and because of his idle time, he desired Bathsheba, which got her pregnant and resulted in having her husband killed in battle.[184] When problems are caused by our sin, we have to live with the consequences as King David did. We read in Psalm 51 King David's prayer to ask for forgiveness after his sin with Bathsheba by recognizing he had sinned against God. It is because of sin that we live in a broken world, and no one is exempt from the problems

---

[182] II Samuel 13:1-39
[183] II Samuel chapter 15-19
[184] II Samuel chapter 11-12

caused from sin. Not even King David, who was a man after God's own heart.[185]

Joseph had many problems he went through in the process to be used of God to save his people from famine, but he trusted God through all of them. The benefit of these problems took Joseph from a spoiled boy to a man who was respected and honored. Moses had many problems accomplishing God's mission of getting the Israelites free from Egypt, plus getting them across the desert to the promised land. The problems that came into Moses' life had taken him from someone unsure of himself to becoming a great leader. Joshua probably had many problems as he continued to lead God's people for Moses, but he was faithful to the end. Joshua, in his old age before his death, reminded his people that all the promises God had given them did come true, plus he gave them a warning for the future.[186] Quite often, like the Israelites, we are impatient to wait on the Lord, and we make our own problems, which takes us longer to receive God's promises. The disciples had many problems as they carried out the Great Commission for Jesus, but their problems made them even stronger in their faith. Even though we cannot see certain results right away, we need to trust that God is in control and will work everything for good.[187] That means things won't always turn out the way we think they should. Although God knows the future, so we can rest in the fact that He will make the right decision for us. Some of our problems can be anything from daily problems to financial problems, health concerns, death in the family, or suffering in some way for our faith. God does not cause our problems but allows us to go through them, but He helps us

---

[185] I Samuel 13:14
[186] Joshua 23:14-16
[187] Romans 8:28

through them. Problems are caused by the circumstances of life in this world or our own choices, but God won't let anything go to waste but serve as a purpose in our lives. God can use the problems that come into our lives to help us to trust Him, help us to grow spiritually, and give us ministry opportunities.[188]

The key is not to look at the problems but to look to "Jesus, the author and perfecter of our faith." [189]

---

[188] Proverbs 3:5-6, Romans 5:1-5, Philippians 1:12-14
[189] Hebrews 12:1-2

DIGESTION PROBLEMS

Problems are a part of life and one of the major health concerns in North America is digestive problems. When I owned a health food store that was one of the main concerns of the people that came in the store for advice. There are many types of digestive issues, such as acid reflux, heartburn, constipation, and irritable bowel, to name a few. We are going to look at how the digestive tract works, why the problems, and how to help.

Digestion is important for breaking down food into nutrients, which the body uses for energy, growth, and cell repair. Food and drink must be changed into smaller molecules of nutrients before the blood absorbs them and carries them to cells throughout the body. First, your digestion starts with smell and taste. Although the process basically starts with your mouth producing your saliva, which helps break down what you are eating because as you chew, it produces enzymes to help absorb nutrients. Once your food is broken down from saliva and chewing, it moves through your esophagus, which is the pipe that connects your mouth to your stomach. After food enters your stomach, the stomach muscles mix the food and liquid with digestive enzymes. Then, the stomach slowly empties its contents into your small intestine. The small intestine is narrower than the large intestine and is actually the longest section of your digestive tube, measuring about 22 feet (or seven meters). Then, the muscles in the small intestine transport food and waste products that allow food to move more smoothly through the digestive tract. Most nutrients are absorbed in the small intestine, where food is broken down even more by enzymes released from the pancreas and bile from the liver. Anything left in the small intestine moves into the large intestine, which is also known as the colon. The colon is a 5 to 7 feet long muscular tube that transfers the remains of the small intestines. Then the colon processes the remains of the small intestines and then sends it into the rectum, which sends it out through the anus. On average, it takes about 36 hours for waste, or stool, to get through the colon. When people think of the colon, they think it just gets rid of waste, but it does so much more. There are good bacteria in the colon that perform several useful functions, such as protecting against harmful bacteria that break down various vitamins and food particles. The colon also performs an essential role by absorbing water, vitamins, and electrolytes from waste material before processing waste products to send out as stool. In the study of embryology, they teach that the colon is the first thing to form in the embryo, and all the major organs sprout from it. That makes the colon the main reflex point for the whole body, which means your body is only as healthy as the condition of your colon.

If you are not eating a healthy diet and drinking plenty of water, it is almost impossible to have a healthy digestive tract. When you eat nutrient-dense foods as your main diet, it will show up as indigestion, acid reflux, constipation, and diarrhea, to name some of the main symptoms. Examples of nutrient-dense foods are all processed foods, plus most packaged foods have hydrogenated oils, especially chips, crackers, and cookies. Try to avoid a lot of red meat, pork, packaged meat, milk, refined flour, sugars, artificial sweeteners, alcohol, juices, citrus fruits, coffee, and wheat. Eat more fruits and vegetables (raw or steamed), plus dark green leafy vegetables, sprouts, avocado, seeds, nuts, quinoa, brown rice, and sprouted grain breads. It is best to drink either Reversed Osmosis water or pH-filtered water since tap water is very acidic. It is important to keep your body hydrated by drinking 5-8 glasses of water a day, and there are no substitutes for water. To help people see the necessity of drinking water to cleanse the inside of the body, I ask people if they would take a shower in juice. You can put an RO system in your home, and then you won't need to purchase and carry those big heavy jugs of bottled water.

There are supplements you can take if you are having problems with your digestive tract or just to keep it healthy. The most needed supplements are fiber (keeps the colon clean), probiotics (builds good bacteria), and digestive enzymes (breaks down food). As we age, we don't produce as many enzymes, so it is important to start taking enzymes by the time you are 45-50 years old. The exception would be if you are having digestive issues no matter your age, you need digestive enzymes. Aloe Vera juice is good for helping children with digestive issues. Also, Aloe Vera juice is great for all kinds of digestive issues, such as acid reflux and constipation, because it helps the digestive tract heal by balancing pH. To help with every aspect of the body's functions, you can do a full body cleanse 1-2 times a year, which includes a colon cleanse.

STIRRED BUT NOT SHAKEN

"I have set the LORD continually before me; Because He is at my right hand, I will not be shaken."

Psalms 16:8

What is the difference between stirred and shaken? The Oxford Dictionary definition for stirred is to mix something, to move or cause to move slightly. The Oxford Dictionary definition of shaken is to move an object with rapid, forceful, jerky movements. God does not want us to be shaken from our faith, but He does, however, want to stir us up because then we can find our strength in Him, grow in maturity, and sometimes change our direction. As you look at these Bible verses, hopefully, the Holy Spirit will continue to develop your faith so you will not be shaken but stirred up to good works.[190]

David writes two specific examples of things we can do to trust God to strengthen our faith. In Psalm 16:8 it says, "I keep my eyes <u>always</u> on the Lord." This is something most Christians struggle with, particularly during a difficult situation. We see a good example of this when Jesus called Peter to walk on the water to Him in a storm. As Peter walked on the water, his focus was on Jesus, which enabled him to walk on the water in the waves and high winds. It was not until Peter took his eyes off Jesus to look at the circumstances around him that he became scared and began to sink. Although even with Peter's lack of faith, all he had to do was to call out, "Lord, save me," and immediately Jesus went to Peter to stretch out His hand

---

[190] Hebrews 10:24 ESV

162

and took hold of him."[191] This example can be a reminder to us in times of fear and doubt not to look at the circumstances. It is also a comfort to know Jesus can help us through them if we just ask.

In Psalms 55:22, David says, "cast your burdens on the Lord, and He will sustain you; He will never allow the righteous to be shaken." In the Oxford dictionary, the word sustain means to strengthen or support, physically or mentally. God will do this for us when we cast our burdens on Him. We often try to carry our burdens ourselves, but God knows we cannot handle the stress because it will affect us physically and mentally. It's not always easy to let go, but it is a necessary part of our trust in God. Since the requirement in this verse is that you cast your burdens on the Lord, how do we do that practically? You can take your burdens to God every day by going to Him in prayer and leaving them with Him.[192] God wants us to humble ourselves by trusting Him to take care of our troubles "because He cares for you."[193] If you are a Christian living right before God, He promises to never allow the righteous to be shaken. David was known as a man after God's own heart because of his relationship with God. David was humble, respectful, trusting, loving, and obedient to God. He also gave God the recognition deserved in Psalms 51:4 when he was truly repentant and acknowledged he alone had sinned against God. He had a heart to please God and knew what it was to trust God, but he also learned the consequences when he did not obey God's word.[194] As David

---

[191] Matthew 11:22-30 NAS
[192] Philippians 4:6-7
[193] I Peter 5:6-7 NAS
[194] Psalm 32: 3-4

wrote verses in the Psalms, they were from what he learned to be true.

I've heard people say God does not give us more than we can handle, which I don't believe that is completely true if you base it on God's word. Since it says in Philippians 4:13, "I can do all things through Him who strengthens me". Since God is the author of every "good and perfect gift," that means He does not cause the difficult situations, but they are a part of life.[195] When God allows difficult circumstances to stir us up for good, it can sometimes feel like we are being shaken when things seem hard to handle, but we can get our strength from God when we draw near to Him. When we keep our eyes on Jesus, we can "walk by faith not by sight" and remember God allows us to be stirred up to accomplish His will for us to be more like Jesus.[196]

The Bible is our foundation that builds our trust in God so that our faith will not be shaken. As it tells us in Psalm 62:2, "He only is my rock and my salvation; My stronghold; I shall not be greatly shaken."

---

[195] James 1:17 NAS
[196] II Corinthians 5:7 NAS

STIR OR SHAKE PROTEIN POWDER

Protein powder is a good illustration of the difference in what happens when you stir or shake something. Most people use or have tried protein powder at some time to get more protein in their diet. Have you ever tried to stir protein powder in your glass and found it does not mix well? Yet you can take that same protein powder and put it in a shaker container, and after it has been shaken, it is mixed well. The reason is that shaking is a harsh process that the protein powder needs to make it break down. In the process of shaking, the protein powder loses its own shape and texture, so it can blend better. Stirring just moves the protein powder around, so it does not completely lose its form when blended. Even though protein powder was a good illustration to compare to stir or shake, we are going to look at a different aspect of the important role protein plays in our body for overall health.

Proteins are essential to every living organism. Next to water, protein makes up the largest proportion of our body. Protein can be found in every single cell in your body, from your hair to muscles, down to the toenails. Your body can manufacture some of its own proteins, but it has to get others from food sources. Proteins are made from building blocks called amino acids. The essential amino acids that the body cannot make on its own can only be provided by food. Such as animal protein because it is the most easily absorbed by the body. Foods that contain all nine essential amino acids are called complete proteins. These foods include beef, poultry, fish, eggs, dairy, soy, quinoa, and buckwheat. Your body uses essential amino acids to produce nonessential and conditional aminos, which are helpful in times of stress or illness. Protein in food provides 4 calories per gram, and current guidelines call for about 2-3 servings of protein-rich foods per day for an adult. Active athletes may require more protein to repair cells.

It is commonly believed that dietary protein is only obtained through animal sources. Surprisingly, to most people, vegetables, nuts, seeds, legumes, and grains are considerable sources of dietary protein and even dark green leafy vegetables. Unfortunately, most people's diets have meat at the center of their meals. There are plenty of reasons to eat more meat-free meals, such as they are cheaper and lower in calories, and the main one would be the balance of pH in the body. A measure of acidity or alkalinity of the fluid in the body needs to be balanced. All meats are acidic, forming in the body, which causes various diseases if the body becomes too acidic.

When you can't get enough protein in a meal or want to replace a meal, you can use protein powder to make a delicious smoothie. You have a choice of Whey, Vegetarian, and Vegan protein. Whey protein is sourced from dairy, and some people don't tolerate dairy, so they can go with vegetarian. I prefer vegetarian protein because it is easier for me to digest but there are some people who want to stay away from all animal sources, and they go with vegan protein.

THE GOOD SHEPHERD

"The LORD is my shepherd. I will have everything I need."

Psalm 23:1 NLV

It is believed that David wrote Psalm 23 later in his life as King. It seems that David was reflecting back on the responsibilities of being a shepherd with the perspective of being a sheep and how God takes care of him as his personal shepherd. It was not easy being a shepherd in Judea because the area was hilly, with no lush green grass except in the rainy season. So, the shepherd would have to take the sheep into the countryside away from home to find grass with the possibility of encountering dangerous wild animals. In those days in Judea, the shepherd did not round up the sheep from behind but would lead them. In a family, it was the youngest son who would become the shepherd, so David was probably around 10 years old when he began his duties as a shepherd. As a shepherd, David had many years of experience in knowing how to take good care of his sheep. At the age of 15, David was anointed by Samuel to be the future King, but he didn't become King until he was 30 years old. Even before David became king, he had many difficult situations in his life to put his trust in God. While we read this study, we can also think of ourselves as being sheep with God as our Shepherd to lead us through our lives. Maybe this can give you a new perspective on how to trust God to be able to say, "I have all that I need."

In verses 1-3, David's message is about God, which is summarized in the first verse, "The Lord is my shepherd" which acknowledges God as the one who provides, protects, and guides him like a shepherd. There was a time in my life when I raised sheep for a few years and found they are not dumb as most people think. Instead, sheep are fearful and need someone to look after them. If you have raised sheep, you would know that they can't be made to lay down in the pasture. Sheep will only lay down when they feel satisfied with provisions and protected in their surroundings, to feel comfortable lying down to rest. When we trust God to take care of all our needs, then we can find peace to rest in Him. The shepherd also knows the sheep are afraid of fast-moving water, so he will lead them to still waters to enable them to get the freshwater they need. God knows our fears so as we trust God to provide and protect, we will find provisions in Him that will restore our soul. When we trust God is in control to guide us, then we will follow Him which will lead us to live a righteous life that will glorify Him.

In verses 1-3, David is talking about the benefits with God as his Shepherd. Then, in verses 4-6, David is now talking to God personally to acknowledge all He does for him as his shepherd. David is telling of his fears but proclaiming to God that he trusts Him for protection, especially in the scary times. There actually is a place in the Judean wilderness called the "Shadow of Death" that is traveled on from Jerusalem to get to Jericho, which David probably walked many times. It is a path that is in a steep, dark, narrow canyon area where the sun only reaches it when directly overhead. There is no one that lives in the area except wild animals, which makes it an even more dangerous path to walk. David may have used the illustration of the "shadow of death" when he walked through dark and uncertain times in his life. The Shepherd always carried a rod that had a short, heavy club end and a slingshot to fight off wild animals. He also had a staff that was a long, thin stick to help with walking on the rocky ground, and he would also use it to reach out to guide the sheep. Then, sometimes, he had to use the hook-shaped end around the neck of a sheep to redirect it. David used the illustration of the rod and staff as a comfort because he knew God was always with him to protect and guide Him like a shepherd would for his sheep with his rod and staff. Then David says to God, "Thou does prepare a table for me in the presence of my enemies," which could be how he always provided for the sheep even though there was always the threat of wild animals looking on. For Christians, this is a good picture of God's care for us as a host that has a personal relationship with us at the table where He provides for us to enjoy. Even though evil ones surround us, they cannot take away what God has provided for us for eternity. The Shepherd used oil for healing the sheep and in the Old and New Testament it is used for healing people from sickness. Although in the Old Testament being anointed with oil also represented God's Blessings for them to be set apart for the work God had for them, just as God sets believers apart.[197] The statement my cup overflows gives us a picture that we are supplied with more than our needs. David believes God's goodness and love will be with him no matter the circumstances in life here on earth. David, as well as Christians, have the hope to be in heaven with God forever!

Calling God our Good Shepherd acknowledges He is good and is concerned about taking care of all our needs in a way that is best for us like the shepherd does for his sheep. When we surrender to God's will and trust Him, He can give us a different perspective of how He provides, protects, and guides us. As we surrender to the will of God, then He can "supply all your needs according to His riches in glory in Christ Jesus".[198]

Since Jesus is the Good Shepherd of our soul, we can say, "I have all that I need".

---

[197] I Peter 2:9
[198] Philippians 4:19 NAS

ALOE VERA JUICE IS GOOD FOR
EVERY HEALTH NEED

Just like the Good Shepherd takes care of his sheep, there are many benefits of using Aloe Vera, which can take care of your body. Most people know it for being one of the best ways to soothe sunburn because, in gel form, it feels like a cool balm for hot skin and is very healing for all burns. However, God has given us the Aloe Vera plant for so many other benefits for our health.

The Aloe plant is considered an herb with spiked-shaped leaves that grow mainly in the dry regions of Africa, Asia, Europe, and America. It has been a popular medicinal plant that people have used for thousands of years as juice

or gel. Each fleshy green leaf contains a slimy tissue that stores water, that makes the leaves thick so the plants can adapt to the hot, dry conditions. The slimy protective tissue is used as the gel for mainly healing externally. The juice water is used to heal internally. There is also a whole plant leaf mulched into a juice for healing internally that is believed to be more effective. Also, animals in the desert will eat the leaves for the water. My favorite Aloe juice is called Georges, which I recommend to everyone has no bitter taste like most Aloe Vera juices. The company printed on their label a story about what they learned during their research in Mexico and Texas, as they observed Roadrunners consistently run to the same type of Aloe plant. Then, they decided to process the leaves on that particular plant with a unique process that makes it appear and taste like water.

Aloe Vera is known for its antibacterial, antiviral, and antiseptic properties. This is part of why the gel heals wounds and treats skin problems as well as first and second-degree burns. It is great to hydrate with it by drinking it alone or putting it in smoothies. You also reap some of the benefits because it is an antioxidant, which is a substance that helps reduce harmful diseases in the body. It is packed full of beta carotene, which your body converts to vitamin A, which is linked to overall eye health. It also contains Vitamin C, which helps with immune function, as well as calcium for bones and magnesium, which helps muscles.

Rinsing your mouth with Aloe Vera juice balances the pH in the mouth. You can use Aloe Juice instead of mouthwash each day because it is effective in killing the plaque-producing bacterium in the mouth, as well as yeast. It can also prevent or heal cancer sores. You can take it to help digestion because of the active enzymes it contains that aid in digestion and help break down fats and sugars while promoting healthy nutrient absorption. That is also why it has been used as a remedy for diabetes since it may enhance insulin sensitivity and help improve blood sugar management. You can drink Aloe Vera juice if you suffer from acid reflux, indigestion, or irritable bowel (IBS) or you can benefit from drinking Aloe Vera juice just as a prevention. The same qualities that make it good for the digestion system enable it to act as a natural laxative that can treat constipation by drinking 2-4 ounces a day. The anti-inflammatory benefits of Aloe Vera juice are very effective in healing ulcers, too. Aloe juice can be used as directed for eye irritations and injuries. I've made eye drops to use each day with some Aloe to prevent cataracts.

It is amazing that God made the Aloe plant to withstand the heat and sun to protect the plants from within. Although God has provided so much more through the plants by providing water for the animals in the desert plus healing from the effects of the sun.

Hopefully, these health tips about Aloe Vera will help you take care of all the needs of the body God has entrusted to you.

WOMEN ARE SPECIAL TO GOD

"Then the Lord God said, 'It is not good for the man to be alone; I will make a helper suitable for him."

Genesis 2:18

Woman was made special from the time of creation! In Genesis 2:18, God knew man would be lonely without someone, so He created a woman to be a special helper for man. Then God took a bone from Adam so woman would be a part of man to complete him. Afterwards, in Genesis 2:21-23, Adam is able to give her the special name of woman. God did not create woman to be inferior to man but to have their own uniqueness. God loves both equally because they are His creation. Although, through the centuries, women have been treated differently than God intended. There are many women that are written about in the Bible, some good and some not so good. We are going to look at a few women who trusted God, and in turn, they were used for a special purpose.

In Matthew chapter 1, there were four women named who had a significant part in the bloodline of Jesus. In Genesis chapter 38, there is the story about the first woman in the bloodline named **Tamar.** She married Judah's firstborn son, Er, but he was evil, so God took his life. After the death of Er, Judah followed the law of customs to uphold the duty to the widow without child, and he sent his second son Onan into Tamar to conceive. Onan didn't carry through on his duty, and God had him die for his disobedience. Because of the death of his first two sons, Judah didn't want to give his youngest son to Tamara. Even though Judah's son was old enough to marry Tamar, He told her to wait till his son was older. Judah never intended to carry through, so Tamar ultimately tricked Judah into impregnating her. When Judah found out, he got Tamar pregnant, he realized that she was more righteous than him because it was his duty to hold up the law of customs. Tamar was a faithful daughter-in-law and was willing to fight for her rights. In Joshua Chapter 2, **Rahab** is introduced as a harlot who owned a house built on the outer walls of Jericho. Joshua sent two spies to stay at her house because it was a perfect place to remain anonymous. Rahab feared the God of the spies because she had heard of all the miraculous things done for them after their escape from Egypt. Rahab had come to believe in the spies' God when she said, "The Lord your God, He is God in heaven above and on earth beneath." Rahab asked the spies to spare not only her life but also her family if she promised to hide them. In Joshua chapter 6:23-25, the spies rescued Rahab and her family and took them back to Israel with them. In the list of the genealogy in the Bible, Rahab was the wife of Salmon, who was believed to be one of the spies. For her courageous faith, this woman with a bad reputation was enrolled among the faithful in the Bible.[199] The book of **Ruth** is about a Moabitess named Ruth, who assimilated into the Jewish culture and accepted her husband's Jewish faith as her own. After her husband and father-in-law died, Ruth gave up her own country and family in order to follow her mother-in-law Naomi back to Israel. Boaz was a relative of Naomi's husband and was impressed by Ruth's loyalty to her mother-in-law. Boaz talked with his workers and told them to let Ruth glean grain from the field and protect her from any harm. This way Ruth could safely provide for herself and Naomi. Ruth also proved her loyalty to Naomi when she followed her custom of faith to marry Boaz and to have a child that would carry

---

[199] Hebrews 11:31

on the family name. **Mary**, the mother of Jesus, trusted God in spite of not totally understanding the full extent of her commitment, and that was a great example of her faith. **Tamar** has shown us how God can use the messiness of our sins to bring us to His will of *redemption*. **Rahab's** faith in God brought her to *salvation*. **Ruth,** because of her loyalty and obedience, was accepted as one of *God's chosen people*. **Mary,** by trusting God's plan for her life, allowed her to give birth to Jesus, the Messiah, to complete the bloodline.

Esther and **Deborah** were two unique women God used to accomplish His will. God enabled **Esther** to become the wife of King Ahasuerus in Susa. In the face of adversity, Queen Esther demonstrated amazing courage on a mission to save the lives of her Jewish people. Esther knew if she attempted to speak with the king before he called upon her, that she could be put to death. So, before she went to the king, she asked her uncle Mordecai to have all the Jewish people pray and fast for her, which resulted in the king honoring her request.[200] She was a woman devoted to her faith and her people, but it was Esther's trust in God that gave her the courage to follow through with God's plan. God will also equip you to courageously live out the calling He has placed on your life if you put your trust in Him. God enabled **Deborah**, a wife and a mother, to also be a prophetess, judge, and warrior. She was the only female judge of Israel plus courageous to go into battle to lead and fight with the Israelites to have a victorious battle over the army of Sisera.[201] We learn from Deborah that God can use women in many areas of life as we are devoted to serving Him and wholeheartedly trusting Him with the results.

---

[200] Esther 3:5-4:17
[201] Judges chapter 4

In Jesus' interactions with women, He respected them by making them feel welcome and affirmed them as valued sisters made in God's image. There was even a group of women that followed Jesus as disciples, and the few that were listed were Mary Magdalene, Joanna, Susanna, and Jesus' mother.[202] As Paul begins Romans 16, he lists women who played a pivotal role in the early church. He first commends Phoebe for serving as deaconess, then goes on to greet other men and women serving in the church. Women also did funding for missionary efforts, opened their homes to Paul plus other apostles, and they had faithful prayer meetings by the river.[203]

A few of the special qualities God has given women are being sensitive, good multi-taskers, and nurturing. God also uses these qualities in the spiritual gifts he has given them. God has made women's characteristics unique from men's, but they are both special to God.

God uses the uniqueness of men and women to work together in different areas of ministry to not be in competition but to complement each other.

---

[202] Luke 8: 1-3, Acts 1:13-14
[203] Romans 16: 1-16, Acts 16:13-15

IS CHOCOLATE OR COFFEE SPECIAL

As we were talking about women being special, it made me think about how special chocolate is to women. Coffee is probably second, but I wonder if men love coffee even more. We are going to look at the benefits and side effects of chocolate and coffee for your health.

Milk Chocolate Versus Dark Chocolate

Chocolate is a popular product that comes from the cacao tree. It is made from cacao beans, which are the seeds stored in the yellow fruit of the cacao tree. Cacao beans have been eaten for thousands of years, and they are a great antioxidant. Similar to the coffee bean, cacao beans have to be roasted before being turned into chocolate.

There are so many delicious products made from chocolate. The difference between dark chocolate and milk chocolate is milk chocolate has more sugar plus milk and less cacao. The dark chocolate is 70-85% cacao, plus it has a decent amount of fiber, and it loaded with minerals. Dark organic chocolate is better for you because it is a good antioxidant, no milk, and a lower amount of sugar. The sugar that added is unprocessed cane sugar, which is lower on the glycemic index. The amount of caffeine in dark chocolate is low compared to coffee. All chocolate should be eaten in moderation, too, because of the sugar.

It seems there is a large amount of coffee drinkers all over the world. No matter how much you love coffee it is important to recognize that caffeine is an addictive substance. Ask yourself, can you go without coffee and not experience withdrawal symptoms like headaches? The least healthy and most addictive coffee is at coffee shops. because there are synthetic substances added to make the coffee smell and taste better and also make you crave more. There are some potential side effects of coffee overuse because of the caffeine, synthetic substances, and over-processing done to the coffee beans. The side effects can be;

-Diuretic effects deplete vitamins, minerals, and friendly bacteria from the body.
-Stimulates acid production in the stomach for more than an hour.
-*Increases* levels of cholesterol and triglycerides that cause heart disease.
-Stimulates the Central Nervous System which can cause nervousness, irritability, insomnia, restless legs, headaches, and fatigue.
-Weakens the adrenals, which can cause adrenal exhaustion, stress, fatigue, and hypoglycemia.
-Increases the chances of bladder, prostate, ovarian, stomach, and pancreatic cancer.
-Can cause kidney stones and fibrocystic breast.

Even knowing the health concerns, a lot of people don't want to give up the enjoyment of a cup or more of coffee. However, it is nice that there are healthier options to choose from, such as buying your own organic coffee beans to grind to brew at home, and now some specialty coffee shops offer organic coffee. If you want decaffeinated coffee, the caffeine is removed through a process of using unnatural ingredients to get it decaffeinated. Although organic decaffeinated coffee is processed through a natural water process to decaffeinate it. It seems that moderation is the best choice for anything in life, so 1-2 cups a day is a good balance. If you like dark chocolate and organic coffee, you can get dark chocolate-covered coffee beans at the health food store and that is a great source of antioxidants.

Benefits of Organic Coffee

Organic coffee is not treated with pesticides or grown in soil with chemical fertilizers. The soil it is grown in has natural nutrients that add value to the coffee beans.

Dark coffee beans are an antioxidant that can fight cancer-causing effects in the body.

I'm not a coffee drinker, but I love to have some dark chocolate every day!

IT JUST HAPPENED

"Behold, I am the Lord, the God of all flesh; is anything to difficult for me?"

Jeremiah 32:27

Often, we have things happen in our lives that we don't even consider as miracles but just coincidences. When we think of miracles, we think of something dramatic that God does. The biblical use of a miracle is about an action of God that produces a result apart from natural means that points to God as the source. There are 83 miracles in the Old Testament and 80 in the New Testament, but today, some people even wonder if God still does miracles.

First, let's start by looking at miracles in the Old Testament. The very first miracle was in Genesis when God created the heavens and earth and all created beings by speaking them into existence.[204] Also, we read about some well-known stories about miracles from the Old Testament, such as Moses at the Red Sea, Joshua at Jericho, Jonah and the whale, and Daniel in the lion's den.[205] God used miracles in the Old Testament to show Himself to his people by providing help, saving them, teaching them, and fighting off enemies. In the New Testament, the first miracle Jesus performed was at a wedding, turning water into wine.[206] In this miracle, God used Jesus' mother to encourage Him to begin His first miracle,

---

[204]Genesis 1:1-31
[205]Exodus 14:21-22, Joshua 6:1-3, 15-16, Jonah 1:17, 2:10, Daniel 3:19-27,5:31
[206]John 2:1-11

which seems He did to show love and respect for her. One of the symbolic messages in this miracle for me, was water is needed for all humanity to live, and wine symbolizes Jesus' blood that enables us to live forever. Jesus healed, raised people from the dead, cast out demons, walked on water, calmed a storm twice, and He fed hundreds of people from a small portion of food twice with more than enough.[207] Through Jesus' miracles, He performed supernatural acts of limitless compassion revealed absolute authority of power through His words over nature, the human body, over sin, and yet, to the disciples' surprise, Jesus revealed that He was God.[208] Jesus introduced the disciples to their ministry by filling their net with an abundance of fish. He also appeared to the disciples after His resurrection, on the beach where they were fishing and filled their net with an abundance of fish, to explain their new ministry.[209]

When thinking about a personal experience with a miracle, my mind went to a major car accident my family had years ago. We were traveling through Kentucky on the highway, heading to Colorado, pulling a camping trailer with our van. As I was coming down a steep hill, I applied my foot to the brake lightly, and the trailer started jackknifing behind us. I had no experience driving and pulling a trailer, so I was depending on my husband to give me directions. He reached around me to pull the brake for the trailer, but it was seized up, and as he pulled it the handle came off. At that point, there was nothing he could do to help me. In my worry of going over the edge of a cliff, I made the decision to drive over to the medium on the grass, which was probably not a smart choice either. As we drove into the medium, the van flipped onto the passenger side, and then

---

[207] Luke 7:12-21, Mark 6:45-51, Mark 6:35-44
[208] John 14:9-10
[209]Luke 5:4-11, John 21:4-22

the trailer flipped, which left me up in the air and my husband against the broken window on the ground. The first thing I said to my husband was how can we get out of the van since the doors wouldn't open. Next thing that happened was a truck driver was at our front windshield, saying he would cut the windshield to get us out. Then, as he was getting us out, a tow truck driver came and turned the gas off in the camper to prevent it from catching on fire. After we were all out, a pastor came and prayed with us, and the ambulance was there. We just had minor injuries, but my teenage daughter and the dog in the middle row of the van had no injuries at all. The tow truck driver was a Christian and he took us to a hotel, and his wife took my husband an hour away to the airport so he could rent a car. The tow truck driver took our camper and van to his property so we could salvage what we needed to take with us. The next day we went to Walmart to buy a car top carrier to put our belongings in and left for Colorado to meet our sons. When my husband asked the pastor for his business card, he said he didn't have any with him, so we couldn't send him a thank you. Then, we began to wonder if God sent us an angel. Since we don't believe in coincidence, we could see God's hand at work in everything and felt blessed.

I believe we can think of miracles in two distinct categories. The *first* are miracles that are obvious and can only be accomplished through God's power. God's power can also work miracles through our giftings as He did through the disciples.[210] The *second* category of miracles are unseen or not as obvious. This could include such things as God's intervention to prevent an accident, which is something that God can do through angels and sometimes, we have no idea that a miracle even occurred. A miracle occurs when God

---

[210] John 14:12

answers prayers, even when it is not exactly how we prayed. However, He will always answer in a way that is best for us. Since God plays an important part in our lives as believers, we should be able to experience several types of miracles in our everyday life.

I believe as Christians the most important miracle to us is that we were hopeless sinners, and God transferred us from darkness to light through Jesus.[211] That is a miracle that keeps working its wonder in our lives every day!

---

[211] Romans 3:23, Ephesians 5:8

THE MYSTERIES OF ALLERGIES

Miracles are similar to allergies because they are not fully understood, and we have been conditioned to think of both of them in a limited capacity too.

We usually think of allergies such as runny nose, sinus problems, skin rashes, asthma, and hay fever. Although, it can also take forms, such as arthritis, gallbladder disease, unmanageable headaches, Crohn's disease, depression, and other conditions not normally thought of as allergy. Over the course of months and years, allergies can weaken the immune system and cause other life threating disease that can take over in the body. The word allergic implies that the allergenic substance is the cause, but it is only the trigger of the allergic reaction. Even people with food allergies generally have a digestive tract that is not functioning properly, which makes it unable to absorb, transport, and utilize food properly for nutrition. This causes varying degrees of malnutrition in the body because there are fewer nutrients than needed, but an increased workload of the allergic substance begins to wear down the immune system. Over time, these functions become more impaired, and the allergic person can become more prone to other diseases. The usual advice given to a person with allergies is to avoid the substance, which can tend to bring relief, but it doesn't get to the root of the problem.

There are three most commonly overlooked conditions that lead to allergies. *Candida Albicans, which* is a yeast like fungus which normally exist in small colonies in the intestinal tract, along with beneficial bacteria and other microbes in a state of balance. However, if this balance is disrupted, Candida may invade other tissue and become an overgrowth that is capable of causing other chronic conditions, as well as serious diseases. Things that can become a contributing factor are medications, antibiotics, chemotherapy, stress, alcohol, coffee, sugar, dairy, gluten, and a poor diet since they kill off good bacteria in the digestive tract. Symptoms might be yeast infections, chronic fatigue, brain fog, poor digestion, food sensitivities, and joint pain. Supplements that can help to treat Candida can be found at your local Health Food store, along with a Candida cleanse. Plus, you need to concentrate on what you eat by lowering your sugar intake and going on a Candida diet. Also, support the liver with a Milk Thistle Formula, a 100 billion probiotic to build up a healthy intestinal tract, and a fiber drink or pills plus lots of water every day to draw out toxins and keep the bowels moving. Another condition is *Parasites*, which most people don't think about because we live in a clean environment. However, if your colon doesn't have a healthy balance of friendly bacteria, it gives the parasites a good environment to live in. The most common types of parasites are different types of worms that you can come in contact with through pets, food, water, and soil. Symptoms can be abdominal pain, diarrhea, gas, bloating, fatigue, and itching around the rectum. With Parasites, you need to do parasite cleansing for two weeks, along with daily fiber, 100 billion probiotic capsule and stay on a low-sugar diet. *Digestive difficulties* are a very important sign because they appear to proceed without conscious awareness. In fact, digestion is the cornerstone of good nutrition because without good digestion, nutrients cannot reach the cells to nourish the body, and a compromised digestive tract leads to allergies. It is one of the most common ailments affecting North Americans today because of poor food choices, too much food, over-processed food, and chemicals in foods that damage the digestive tract. Some diseases that are caused are heart disease, obesity, alcoholism, cancer, diabetes, stroke, arthritis, mental illness, and high blood pressure. The changes you can make to prevent or help with digestive issues is to eat a good balanced organic diet with fruit, lots of vegetables, less meat, and good digestive enzymes with each meal. You also can add a green food supplement, aloe vera juice, probiotics, and fiber to add support for the digestive tract.

I have been helping people with digestive issues for over 25 years and have learned a lot along the way. I would recommend reading the book called "Allergies Disease in Disguise" written by Carolee Bateson-Koch, DC, ND. This book helped me to understand more of the disease side of allergies and could be helpful for you to read if you have allergies.

ANGELS

"Are they not all ministering spirits, sent out to render service for the sake of those who will inherit salvation?"

Hebrews 1:14

Secular culture was heavily focused on angels in the 1990s, on television, books, and angel items being sold. However, not with a proper focus on their true purpose. There are around 300 places in the Bible where Angels are mentioned. Even though God created angels to play an important part in the life of Christians, they were not meant to be made more important than God. Angels were created with different purposes that we will discover as we look into God's word.

We first encounter angels when they were created in Genesis 2:1 when it says, "Thus the Heavens and the earth were completed, and all their hosts." In Colossians 1:16, Paul includes the angelic world when he says that God created all things "visible and invisible, whether thrones or dominions or principalities or authorities". In Matthew chapter 26:53, Jesus is in the garden of Gethsemane and is being arrested by the chief priests and elders. One of his disciples reached out to attack the soldiers arresting Jesus, and He stopped him and said, "do you think that I cannot appeal to My Father, and He will at once put at my disposal more than twelve legions of angels?" To give some perspective on the size of what this would have looked like, a legion in military terms is equal to 6,000 men. In 1 Samuel 17:45-50, God is called the Lord of host, which means He is the commander of Angels. Jesus did not want the angels to protect

Him because He chose to continue to follow God's will to the cross. In the Bible, they are referred to as spirits, which would mean they would not have physical bodies like ours. After Jesus' death and resurrection in Luke 24:36-39, he appears to the disciples, and they think He is a spirit. However, Jesus invites them to touch His hands and feet to see He is human and not spirit.

Whenever an angel is called the Angel of the Lord, it refers to Jesus, plus the person who sees Him will always bow down and call Him my Lord. Angels cannot usually be seen by humans unless God reveals them, as He did with Balaam and his donkey.[212] When Elisha prayed to God that he would open the eyes of his servant so he could see the angels that were fighting the battle for them.[213] There are several examples in scripture where angels took on the bodily form of a human and appeared to people. One such story involves Abraham, as he was sitting at his tent door, he looked up and saw three men, so he ran from the tent door to meet them. Then he asked them to stay as he washed their feet and got them some food.[214] Hebrews 13:2 tells us, "Do not neglect to show hospitality to strangers, for by this some have entertained angels without knowing it." Angels in scripture are often referred to as a bright light, such as when an angel came to get Peter out of jail, "a light shone in the cell."[215] When Cornelius was praying, a "man stood before him in shining garments", and the angel told him to find Peter. When Peter went to Cornelus's house, Cornelus fell on his face to worship Peter, but Peter made him stand up and told Cornelus he was just a man.[216] In Revelation 7:11 it says the angels are around God's throne, so it would seem because they are in the presence of the glory of God, it is probably why they shine.

---

[212] Numbers 22:20-35
[213] II Kings 6:15-17
[214] Genesis 18:1-5
[215] Acts 12:7 NAS
[216] Acts 10:17-30 NAS

The *cherubim* and *seraphim* are the angels that appear with God in heaven. *Cherubim* are the most frequently occurring heavenly creatures in the Bible, as they appear around 91 times. Cherubim means a celestial winged being who represents God's spirit on Earth and symbolizes the worship of God. In Genesis 3:24, God placed Cherubim to guard the entrance to the Garden of Eden after the fall of man. They were also in Ezekiel's vision when he saw them in heaven.[217] Two gold cherubim were placed on the Ark of the Covenant as a symbol of God's presence on earth.[218] The name *seraph* means burning one or shining one, probably since they are in God's presence, and they show reverence to God by covering their face with their wings. The *seraphim* are only mentioned once in Isaiah 6:1–7 when Isaiah saw a vision of heaven, and it seems the seraphim's main purpose is to continually worship God. Two important angels we read about in the bible are *Gabriel* and *Michael*. *Gabriel* appears as a messenger to people for good news. As he appeared to Zechariah for the birth of John, he spoke to Mary before Jesus' birth, and he also appeared to Daniel regarding his prayer.[219] *Michael's* role is that of protecting and fighting. In Jude he was called an archangel, which means he was the highest in highest rank in the army of angels. In Daniel 10:13 Michael was called to fight off the prince (demon) of Persia so Daniel's prayer could be answered.

Even though angels are mentioned many times in the Bible, it only explains the importance of why God created them. God has not only created them to worship Him but to protect us and fight our spiritual battles.

---

[217] Ezekiel chapter 10
[218] Exodus 25:17-20
[219] Daniel 9:21-22

Even though we are not to worship angels, I believe it is good to thank God for creating them to play an important role in our lives as believers.

THE UNKNOWN ABOUT CHOLESTEROL

When it comes to angels, most people don't really understand who they are and what their real purpose is. It is the same way with cholesterol because there are so many misunderstandings about the purpose of cholesterol and what causes it.

We are told that we need to watch our cholesterol in order to prevent a heart attack or stroke. Yet numerous studies have shown that 75% of all heart attack patients' cholesterol levels were actually normal, as stated in the American Heart Journal (January 2009). New studies have also shown that heart attack and stroke are not the link between bad cholesterol as being the main cause as previously thought.

Most of the cholesterol circulating in the body is made within the body and does not come from the foods you eat. The body makes cholesterol because it is needed for many functions in the body. The cholesterol molecule is utilized in the production of many hormones such as testosterone, progesterone, and Vitamin D. It is needed for keeping the cells healthy and for assisting the body in digesting other forms of fat.

Cholesterol doesn't cause heart attacks, but the oxidized form of cholesterol is one of the significant components of the substance that makes up arterial plaque. Merely reducing the amount of cholesterol in your blood has no relationship to the oxidation of cholesterol or the laying down of plaque in the arteries. Plaque happens because of injury to the artery wall, and the injury is caused by sugar sticking to the protein fibers that make up the artery. The artery is injured by oxidation, which is caused by sugar produced from trans fats, which contributes to inflammation and is responsible for the continued laying down of plaque in the arteries.

The worst offenders are margarine and shortening, which are trans fats. Most of the trans fats found in the typical Canadian diet come from margarine, fried foods, bakery products made from shortening, and hydrogenated oils. The foods they are found in include crackers, cookies, donuts, cakes, pastries, muffins, croissants, snack foods, french fries, and breaded foods. Some of the food companies are trying to cut back on trans fats, but when companies print their product label to say it is zero trans fats is misleading. Food guidelines only specify that these foods have less than half a gram of trans fats per serving and that the serving size is much smaller than an average person would consume. So, it is always good to read the labels.

Satin drugs are one of the most popular classes of drugs prescribed for cholesterol worldwide. Satin drugs can cause side effects, including muscle pain, liver damage, increased blood sugar, memory loss, and sexual dysfunction. Cholesterol-lowering medications interfere with the body's production of a very important molecule called Co-enzyme Q10. This nutrient is necessary for energy production in the body and is particularly abundant in the muscles. Since the heart is the most important muscle in the body, lower levels in the heart are associated with increased weakness of the heart and, therefore, higher incidences of congestive heart failure. Vital organs such as the liver and kidneys may also suffer from these drugs.

Foods that encourage healthy arteries are foods high in antioxidants, good fats, and fiber. Some of these foods are such things as vegetables, fruit, greens, seeds, nuts, berries, avocado, broccoli, and dark chocolate. Most supplements that are helpful are also good antioxidants, good fats, and fiber. Some supplements that are helpful are Vitamin K2, CoQ10, Niacin, Vitamin C (high doses), Lysine, garlic, Sunflower Lecithin, Fish Oils, Red Rice Yeast, Hawthorne, and supplemental fiber.

ARE WE THERE YET?

"Wait for the LORD; Be strong, and let your heart take courage; Yes, wait for the LORD."

Psalms 27:14

Years ago, when our children were younger, we would take long trips in the car to the United States. As we traveled, they would usually ask the same question more than once, "Are we there yet?" One of the hardest things for people to do is wait! However, when you think of it, there are a lot of activities that we need to do that require us to wait. Some examples would be going to restaurants, movies, concerts, sports games, airports, and grocery checkout lines, just to name a few. One of the hardest places to wait is the doctor's office because we usually don't feel well, and usually the wait is very long. I guess that is why we are called patients! Waiting can seem like a waste of time, but it is the process we must go through to acquire what we need or want.

God knows that we are impatient people, and that is probably why there are seventy-one verses in the Bible that talk about waiting. We usually want to charge ahead to take control of difficult situations in our lives. In Psalms 27:14, David repeats "wait for the LORD" two times to help instill the importance of waiting for God. He also instructs us to be strong so we can withstand the pressures in our lives with God's strength. When we read our Bible, it reassures us to stand firm in God's promises, such as Isaiah 40:31, which gives us a promise that if we wait on the LORD, we will "gain new strength". After Moses died, God asked Joshua to take the Israelites across the Jordan River into the Promised Land. God reminded Joshua to be strong and courageous and not to fear because He was with him wherever he went, which is also a promise for us.[220] Psalms 31:24 says, "Be strong, and let your heart take courage, All you who wait on the LORD." When we are asked to take courage, it is because we are doing something that frightens us, but if we are waiting on the LORD, He will enable us to do it. While we confidently wait for the LORD to act on our behalf, we can bring our request to Him in prayer, stand firm on His promises, and go to Him with hearts of thanksgiving and praise.[221] Even though we don't like those difficult times of waiting we can trust that God has a purpose for us in the wait.[222]

There is a great illustration of the purpose of waiting in the book of Acts when Jesus told the disciples to wait in Jerusalem for the Holy Spirit. I believe God wanted to accomplish a few things in the Apostles' lives as they waited for the Holy Spirit.[223] "*First,*" Jesus commanded the Apostles not to leave Jerusalem because they needed to be in the place where Jesus wanted them. In the waiting, the Apostles were learning _obedience_. "*Second,*" Jesus asked them to wait for the Holy Spirit that the Father had promised. This would have been difficult for them to understand since the disciples didn't fully realize the purpose of the Holy Spirit yet. In the waiting, they were learning to _trust_ that God would fulfill the promise, and then they would understand the purpose. "*Third,*" Before He ascended, Jesus told the Apostles that it would not be many days before the Holy Spirit would come. The Apostles went to the Upper Room to wait, which turned out to be ten days, so they were learning _patience_. When God tells us to wait, we never know how much time it will be, but we can trust in the fact He has a purpose.[224] "*Fourth,*" it had been a very *emotional time* for the Apostles since they were

---

[220] Joshua 1:9
[221] Philippians 4:6
[222] Romans 5:3-5
[223] Acts 1:4-26
[224] Romans 8:28

not totally prepared for Christ's death, resurrection, and His ascension into Heaven. Maybe some were even feeling the guilt of deserting Jesus at the cross and were overwhelmed with how Jesus extended them forgiveness.[225] The wait was needed for _healing_ for each of the disciples as they reflected on all that happened. "*Fifth*," the Apostles needed the wait for a _resting_ time to give them the strength they would need before the Holy Spirit came to give them a new ministry. During this time, the Apostles didn't just sit around waiting, but they were *active*. They had other disciples join them who were all of *one mind*, devoting themselves to *prayer* every day. Peter also *preached* to a large group of brethren, plus they *chose* Matthias to replace Judas to move forward when ready.[226] It seems during that waiting time, there was an extra bond of *unity* being developed amongst the disciples, too.

God asks us to first *wait* in our circumstances, to *be strong* in His strength, *trust* Him to give us courage of heart, and then He *reminds* us again to wait. Waiting might seem like a difficult thing to do but know that God will accomplish what He wants in you, through you, and for you during the process.[227]

You will find that it will be *worth the wait!*

---

[225] Mark 14:50, Mark 14:66-72
[226] Acts 1:12-26
[227] Proverbs 3:5-6

IMPATIENT WITH COLDS & FLU

The one thing that cold and flu have in common with waiting is that you must wait till the cold or flu gets out of your system. Although in natural health care, you can use prevention to keep from getting sick, and you can also shorten the duration of the cold or flu by using natural supplements. I'm going to give you suggestions on how you can do that.

The common cold affects the upper respiratory tract and consists of inflammation of the mucous membranes of the nose, throat, eyes, and ears. It is medically referred to as a viral upper respiratory tract infection with symptoms that include cough, sore throat, low-grade fever, nasal congestion, runny nose, and sneezing. They are called the common cold because they are common for most people to get because they do not discriminate and can infect everyone in their path. They are communicable and transfer in numerous ways, especially in confined places where the germs could be floating in the air. Most people are confused about the difference between a cold and the flu. Although symptoms of the flu can be similar to a cold because it can have some of the same symptoms, such as fever or feeling feverish/chills, cough, sore throat, runny or stuffy nose, muscle or body aches, headaches, and fatigue. Cold symptoms usually start gradually and are usually milder than the symptoms of flu, which start suddenly and intensely and last longer. Colds generally do not result in serious health problems like the flu, which can cause complications such as pneumonia. Then there is the stomach flu, which is called viral gastroenteritis, which is an intestinal infection marked by watery diarrhea, abdominal cramps, nausea or vomiting, and sometimes fever. Viral gastroenteritis can be deadly for infants, older adults, and people with compromised immune systems because of dehydration. The most common way to develop viral gastroenteritis is through ingesting contaminated food or water. It is easy to confuse viral diarrhea with diarrhea caused by bacteria such as C. difficile, salmonella, E. coli, or parasites.

There are precautions you can take naturally to prevent and fight off colds and flu. Basic actions of things you can do is to make sure you are bundled up in the cold weather with a hat, wash your hands often, especially before you eat, and do not put your fingers in your mouth. Also, avoid confined places if you can, but in some situations, it can be impossible to do, especially if you have small children. There are also immune builders you can take during cold and flu season and other supplements you can purchase from health food stores that can help. Supplements that build up immunity plus help you to fight off cold and flu, such as Ki Immune, Silver, Garlic, Vitamin C, Vitamin D, Zinc, Elderberry, Oil of Oregano, Ki Cold formula, and Black Walnuts for parasites. Also, there are foods we should stay away from that cause inflammation in the body, which makes us more susceptible to colds & Flu and harder to get rid of them. Try to stay away from refined sugars and flours (most packaged foods), candy, cookies, red meat, processed meat, dairy, alcohol, potato chips, pop, acidic fruits, and juices. I know that might seem like a lot to give up, but what is your health worth to you?

MASTERPIECE

"For we are God's masterpiece. He has created us anew in Christ Jesus, so we can do the good things he planned for us long ago."

Ephesians 2:10 (NLT)

What do you think of when you hear the word Masterpiece? When I hear the word Masterpiece, it makes me think of a beautiful painting. The definition of Masterpiece in the Oxford dictionary is a work of outstanding artistry, skill, or workmanship. We are going to look at how God, the ultimate creator of workmanship, has made us a masterpiece.

God's masterpiece began in Genesis chapter 1-2 when He created the earth, all living things, and mankind. When God created mankind, He did not want them to be like robots, so he gave them free will to be able to share companionship with Him. Then sin (not obeying God's way) was brought into the world by Adam and Eve, which was the cause of all mankind being born with a disobedient heart.[228] A good example of where you see sin carried through was with Adam and Eve's son Cain since he killed his brother out of jealousy.[229] God had given Abraham the law long before Moses brought the 10 commandments, but there still continued to be a lot of sin mentioned and following idols in Genesis.[230] It seems that Moses wasn't giving a new law but a formal version of God's law so that it could be used to govern the nation of Israel as they left Egypt. Most people think of God's laws as do's and don'ts to take all the fun out of life, but it really is God's love letter to protect us from the

---

[228] Romans 5:12-13
[229] Genesis 4:1- 8
[230] Genesis 26:4-5

effects of sin. Some people think they can't relate to the 10 commandments because they think they are good enough because they have never killed anyone or done evil things. Although we all probably can relate to a few of these things, we maybe have done at some time, such as stealing, lying, envy, and being prideful. In the New Testament, Jesus defines sin in terms that we can understand.[231] The point is that not all sin is equally wicked, but in God's eyes, all sin is bad because it is being disobedient to Him.[232] Since sin is more of a heart issue, Jesus used the illustration of adultery to prove a point when he said to the people, "that everyone who looks on a woman to lust for her has committed adultery with her already in his heart.[233] Therefore, disobedience has caused division between man and God, and even to this day, we see the effects it has on our lives and in the world God has given us.

We personally became His masterpiece when David writes in Psalm 139:13, "For Thou didst form my inward parts; Thou didst weave me in my mother's womb". We start out wonderfully created as beautiful babies, innocent to the ways of the world but still born with a nature of disobedience passed down from Adam and Eve. Now, we want to look at how God has reached down to us to make a way to correct all this. In Matthew 5:17-18, Jesus said, "Do not think that I have come to abolish the law or the prophets; I have not come to abolish them but to fulfill them". Jesus is talking about the Old Testament, which gave people laws to live by, and prophets that foretold what was to come if they didn't follow the law. Jesus knew the people would still need the law since they would be living in an evil world, and they needed the predictions of the prophets to be prepared for things to come. When Jesus said He had come to fulfill them, it explains how in Romans 3:23, "All have sinned and fall short of the glory of God" and He came to make a way back for us to

---

[231] Mark 7:20-23
[232] James 2:10
[233] Matthew 5:27-28

God. God loved us so much that He made a way for us to be with Him forever through Jesus's death on the cross.[234] Once we confess our sins and accept Jesus as our Lord and Savior, we become children of God.

Therefore, because of what Jesus has done for us, we have become a new creation.[235] Now, because you are a new creation, you have also been set free of sin and death as it says in Romans 8:2, "For the law of the spirit of life in Christ Jesus has set you free from the law of sin and of death". We now have a new heart and want to be obedient to our Father God because we love Him. Life does not become perfect because we are still living in a sinful world, but God will always be with us to strengthen us and help us go through our lives.[236] We are now like a blank canvas that God can create the masterpiece we were intended to be before sin changed things. God is like a potter, changing us by shaping us through trials and circumstances to make us more like Jesus.[237] Paul said, "He who began a good work in you will perfect it until the day of Christ Jesus", which is when we go to heaven or are raptured to be with Him.[238] When we receive Jesus personally, there is no division of people according to our previous lives or the color of our skin. We become a part of the body of believers, which is called the body of Christ.[239]

We are like colorful pieces of broken glass put together in a beautiful Mosaic picture to make up the Body of Christ. This is God's final Masterpiece that He will take to Heaven.

---

[234] John 3:16
[235] II Corinthians 5:17
[236] Isaiah 41:10
[237] Isaiah 64:8
[238] Philippians 1:6 NAS
[239] I Corinthians 12:27

DETOXIFY THE BODY FOR THE PICTURE OF HEALTH

When God created man, everything was perfect, but sin changed everything. That is why we need Jesus to cleanse our sins so we can be the masterpiece God intended. It is similar to our bodies in that they are affected by the environment we live in and our food choices. We can't have control of all the environmental things on the earth that affect our health. However, we can help to protect our health by choosing a natural living environment in our homes, good organic food choices and supplements to give our body a fighting chance. God has given us good organic whole food choices, but it seems easier to choose processed and fast food when we eat. Just as we needed Jesus to purify our body from sin to give us new life, we need to detoxify our body to purify the effects of toxins in our body so we can have a better quality of life while we are on earth.

A simple description of detoxification is cleansing the body on the inside. It is as important as bathing or brushing your teeth. It is one of the most important health-related functions we can perform in our lives, and it is surprisingly easy for us to undertake. Toxicity is a problem that virtually every person has during their lifetime. Toxins come from our air, food, household cleaners, cosmetics, alcohol, prescription drugs, and a variety of other sources. As more toxins accumulate, our bodies are less effective in naturally eliminating those toxins. Toxins in the body contribute to a variety of health issues, which may include allergies, arthritis, cancer, depression, digestive problems, irritable bowel, low energy, low sex drive, mental fog, skin issues, and weight gain or loss. If your body is already struggling with severe health issues it is best to build your body's health up before you detox and then you start slowly on a mild detox first.

In today's toxic environment, the body can deal with tissue acid wastes, mental and physical limitations, chemical and heavy metal residue build-up, that result in a greater incidence of allergies. Numerous products and programs are available to support the body in its natural cleansing process that can help to combat these effects. More alternative health practitioners are introducing detoxification programs to reduce these symptoms and maintain health. There are different types of cleanses available.

- *Herbal Cleanses* can be found at your local Health Food Store. Herbal cleanses are available in liquid or pill form, taken in conjunction with a high fiber, probiotic, natural laxative as needed, nutrient-rich diet, and increased water intake. Typically taken two times a day for 7 days. The herbs help release waste and toxins stored in the digestive system. Plus, there are herbal cleanses for parasites, candidiasis (yeast), and liver that you can do after your main cleanse.

- *Colon Hydrotherapies* is bathing the colon with purified warm water to eliminate the build-up of fecal matter in the colon while also removing excess mucus, bacteria, and parasites present in the waste matter. Hydrotherapies help digestion, promote regular bowel movements, weight loss, immunity, and boost energy.

- *Chelation Therapy* is administering chelating agents to eliminate heavy metals from the body. Due to our environment, our bodies can absorb toxic chemicals and heavy metals such as mercury, lead, arsenic, and aluminum. A Chelation Clinic will do extensive blood and urine samples and send them away to a special blood clinic for a complete report. Then, when the results come back, you can decide if you want treatment. They perform chelation therapy by introducing agents that bond with metal ions through IV treatments. You will have a series of appointments so the toxins and heavy metals can slowly be excreted by the kidneys and eliminated.

Chelation Therapy is helpful in the treatment of fatigue and the risk of heart attack and stroke, it reduces pain and swelling and limits symptoms of Alzheimer's and diabetes. I met a woman who had chelation therapy for diabetes that saved her from needing surgery to remove her foot. I also have a friend who had chelation therapy for his heart condition, and his doctor was impressed by the improvement.

- *Foot Detox* is a gentle foot bath full of water with a bit of salt, with an electrode array that generates charged ions to attract and attach toxic particles so they can be released. By osmosis, toxic particles are pulled from the body through the sweat glands on the bottom of your feet. A session typically lasts 30 minutes and is very relaxing, very safe, effective, and an easy way to detox. It increases blood circulation which supports the health and wellness of your entire body, and can prevent various health problems which are made worse by poor circulation. I gave Ionic Treatments to clients in my store for years. Some of the results that were noticed was better digestion, helped constipation, helped inflammatory conditions like arthritis, and just a better feeling of wellness. I also recommend an oral herbal detox for clients before chelation therapy to help release more toxins.

Many products and services are available, ranging in price and effectiveness. Be sure to do your research and choose the proper detox suited for you. It is best to do two detoxes a year for best results, if you can. You can think of it like Spring and Fall house cleaning. Many times, people start cleaning but do not finish it. Remember, the only good detox to work toward good health is the one that you are going to complete!

RUN THE GOOD RACE

"Run in such a way that you may win."

I Corinthians 9:24

God reminds us in Psalms 139:13-16 that He knew us when we were being formed in our mother's womb and even how many days we will live. In Psalm 90, Moses writes a prayer in which he mentions God's eternity compared to people's temporary lives.[240] Then, in verse 12, Moses asks God to "Teach us to number our days, that we may present to you a heart of wisdom." Since we are uncertain of how many days our life will be on this earth, it would be wise to pray for a heart of wisdom to help us make each day count as if it were our last. This should encourage us to live out our faith in God because "even so faith if it has no works, is dead being by itself".[241] This study is going to look at ideas of how we can use the time God has given us to run and complete the race He has set before us.

As we think of our personal mission to run the good race, it can change throughout our lives. A good example of this is the changes that churches have made through the years. In the past, the church concentrated on the main mission of being in other countries to tell them about Jesus. Now, churches realize missions can be done more effectively by showing them Jesus through their actions as well. This is being done by teaching them skills to be able to take care of their own practical needs and training Christian people in their communities to be pastors. This enables the people to teach their people, then that makes it more relatable and gives them independence. Also, most churches are looking more into practical

---

[240] Psalm 90:4
[241] James 2:17 NAS

ministry in their own communities as mission work that is much needed. Jesus even told the disciples their mission was to receive the Holy Spirit which would enable them to be a witness close to home (Jerusalem, Judea, Samaria) then they could reach out into the world.[242]   Not every Christian is called to missions in another country, and there are a lot of opportunities to serve in outreach through our church. Therefore, no matter what your age, occupation, or where you live, you can have a mission field without leaving your own community. Although, if we have a family, our first ministry should start in our own home, because it is important not to get so busy that we don't have time for family needs. As a mother, it was important for me to reflect the nature of God for our family by creating a loving, cheerful atmosphere with clean and organized surroundings in our home. Also, my husband and I provided the children with spiritual growth by teaching about the Bible, attending church, praying together, talking about how God is taking care of our daily needs, showing care for others, and teaching by example. While making your family a top priority you can also use your giftings in ministry opportunities in the church. We can also minister to our Christian friends throughout the week by keeping in touch by text and e-mails, praying for them, and helping them out when there is a need. Then, of course, there are neighbors outside of the church who we are to love as ourselves, too.[243] This is not just neighbors in our neighborhood but people we routinely see, such as parents from our children's school, children's activities, people who work at stores where we shop, employees of restaurants where we eat, and our mechanic, to name a few. With our closer neighbors, it can be easier to show God's love as we talk with them on our lawns, have them over for a meal, have a barbeque for a few of the neighbors to meet each other, send notes of encouragement, and sometimes they might need help with fixing something or

---

[242] Acts 1:8 NAS
[243] Mark 12:31

taking them a meal in a difficult time. We can also be used by God to show love to complete strangers by helping them out if their car breaks down, help by serving meals at a shelter, giving food and clothing where needed, and buying a homeless person a coffee, meal, or a bus ticket. We should always be prepared to "conduct ourselves with wisdom toward outsiders, making the most of the opportunity" to be available to share our faith with others as we season our speech with grace.[244] We should not let age or disabilities stop us because we can all minister where God has placed us.

When you feel called to ministry in a certain place, and it doesn't work out, don't get discouraged because God has another plan for you. Paul had his missionary trip planned, and he attempted to go into a certain region, but he was prevented from entering because God wanted him in Macedonia to minister to a family there.[245] Therefore, keep in mind things won't always work out as we plan, and there will probably be some pain and sorrow on the way, but we still need to be faithful.[246] Despite our circumstances, "whatever you do, do all to the glory of God".[247]

The Bible is full of God's promises that He is in control. So "let us run with endurance the race set before us, fixing our eyes on Jesus," till God calls us home when our race is finished and says well done good and faithful servant.[248]

---

[244] Colossians 4:5-6 NAS
[245] Acts 16:6-10
[246] James 1:2
[247] I Corinthians 10:31 NAS
[248] Hebrews 12:1-2 NAS, Matthew 25:21

MOVEMENT WITH ARTHRITIS & OSTEOPOROSIS

As we get older, there will be more health issues that can limit us as we run the good race, such as arthritis and Osteoporosis. However, we can continue to run the good race that is honoring to God no matter the circumstances as he continues to enable us.

Osteoporosis is specifically a condition dealing with the minimization of bone density, which usually affects women over fifty. Arthritis is the swelling and tenderness of one or more of your joints. The main symptoms of arthritis are joint pain and stiffness, which typically worsen with age. An injured or overused joint is more likely to develop arthritis, as I have found from overworking my wrist shoveling and falling last year on my arm. The most common types of arthritis are osteoarthritis and rheumatoid arthritis. Osteoarthritis occurs when the smooth cartilage joint surface wears out and Rheumatoid arthritis is an autoimmune disease, which means that the immune system malfunctions and attacks the body. Arthritis affects the joints, so the pain is usually limited to the knees, hands, hips, and possibly the spine and are also areas where fractures have occurred, like in Osteoporosis. One thing people do not consider is Osteoporosis and Arthritis are primarily lifestyle diseases. Genetics only play a minor role because a stressful life, depression, smoking, prescription drugs, and not eating a balanced diet all contribute to more inflammation in the body, which can cause both conditions. Also, keeping an active lifestyle and exercising are important for prevention. Some of the best forms of exercise are low-impact activities like brisk walking, biking, and even gardening, which have been proven to be the best way to increase bone density. When you can't get outside, for convenience, you can use a stationary bike, treadmill, or rebounder (mini trampoline). They are all excellent sources of exercise that is great for circulation.

Osteoporosis is an inflammatory condition in the body that is caused when the body becomes acidic. The body tries to balance the acid condition by taking the calcium and minerals from the bones to neutralize the acidic body. Arthritis is caused by acidic conditions in the body that solidifies the calcium in the body, depositing calcium in the joints, and they become inflamed and ache. It is assumed that we need to take calcium supplements, but they can also cause problems like depositing excess calcium in the kidneys, arteries or upsetting the stomach. Calcium tablets make it difficult for the digestive system to break them down. Most times the tablets even leave the body without absorption and go directly into the septic system. A calcium supplement is more effective in liquid form or homeopathic mineral tabs to dissolve in your mouth. Women have been told for years to take large doses of calcium for Osteoporosis but now it has been realized that we need more magnesium than calcium for better absorption to strengthen the bones. The best form of magnesium is to take a powder, which you need to boil water to dissolve and activate it. Along with supplements, you can absorb calcium from natural food sources in your diet, such as vegetables and dark leafy greens. In the past, it was also the practice to recommend dairy products to increase calcium intake. However, research shows that a higher intake of dairy products can cause a greater risk of developing osteoporosis. The milk is overprocessed, and ingredients are added that cause more inflammation in the body. It is inaccurate to assume that any food that contains high amounts of calcium will adequately be digested to extract the minerals needed and store them in the body. Although a healthy diet with certain supplements is good to combat and ease Osteoporosis and arthritis by making the body more pH balanced to keep inflammation down.

All high-protein foods, especially meat and dairy products, make the body acidic, which draws calcium out of the bones. You can eat a healthy diet to keep inflammation down in the body by not eating inflammatory foods such as animal protein, dairy, refined sugars, trans fats, margarine, refined flours, pastas, breads, cereals, desserts, acidic fruits, and juices. It is good to read labels on food, which can help you be aware of refined sugars, additives, trans fats, and other harmful ingredients. Our diet should consist of 80% alkaline foods, and the majority of those are vegetables (especially green leafy), brown rice, good grains, chia, hemp, seeds, and nuts. You can Google pH food charts that list acidic and alkaline foods to help you make the right food choices. Plus, you can take anti-inflammatory supplements such as greens, fish oil, curcumin, vitamin E, zinc, and B-12. Magnesium is very important in helping bones to absorb calcium, Silica builds collagen. These supplements lead to greater flexibility in the bones, help form new bones, and strengthens mature bone.

THE GOD OF THE OLD TESTAMENT

A friend of mine recently said, "The God of the Old Testament is so mean." I understand where she was coming from since many people have this misconception of God. I explained to her that the God of the Old Testament is the same God in the New Testament because He never changes, and His love for His people can be read throughout both books. Since God is truth, He chose real people to write about, not made-up stories. I find reading the Old Testament helpful because it is about real people dealing with various struggles and a reminder for us of the difference it makes when we choose to be obedient and trust God. It is important to remember that from the beginning of creation, Adam and Eve chose to be disobedient to their Father God. Therefore, because of their disobedience, all people inherited a sinful nature and will reap the consequences of sin. When people choose to be disobedient to God, they often blame God for being harsh and mean.

There are significant differences in the Old Testament because people lived by the law of sacrifices to pay for their sins. In the New Testament, after Jesus died as a sacrifice for sins, it gave people the choice to live by grace instead of the law, and that would enable them to no longer be slaves to sin. In the Old Testament, people who were obedient to God could receive the Holy Spirit for ministry, but only as needed. In the New Testament, when people accept Jesus, the Holy Spirit stays with them forever. We are going to look at a few verses in the Old Testament to see how God showed love for His people.

In *Genesis,* after Adam and Eve chose to sin, God took compassion and clothed them with the first animal sacrificed to make garments of skin for them.[249] In *Exodus,* God helped His people leave Egypt

---

[249] Genesis 3:1-24

plus showed them favor through the Egyptians as they sent His people away with silver, gold, and clothing for their future. Even when Pharoh and his men decided to chase the people with Chariots, God protected them by parting the red sea for them to cross.[250] While in the wilderness, God led them with a pillar of cloud in the day, a pillar of fire by night and provided food and water for them. God gave them the 10 commandments to give them laws to live by in the Promised Land. These laws would provide them with a standard to live by to guide them to make the right choice so it would protect them from the effects of sin on their life.[251] God told Moses to make Joshua his successor when he died so he could take the people into the Promised Land. God instructed the people how to cross the Jordon River, and He parted the water for them again.[252] In the Promised Land, after Joshua's death, the people had no leader, and they began doing what was right in their own eyes and began to sin again. Then God gave the people *Judges,* who were enabled by the Spirit to deliver the people, secure rest in the land, and promote obedience to the commandments. Yet the people still rebelled against God, so because of that, He did not drive out the nations that would harm them. God also gave them *Prophets* to be the divine voice of God on earth, and *Samuel* was the first prophet,[253] and the last Judge. When Samuel grew old, the people demanded that he find them a king. God held the position as their king, so Samuel went to Him for advice to know how to respond. God instructed Samuel what to say as a warning of how their life would change when ruled by a king, but they preferred a King over God.[254]

---

[250] Exodus 12:35-36, Exodus 14: 21-16
[251] Exodus 13:21, 16:12, 17:6, 20:1-17
[252] Numbers 27:16-17, Joshua 3:7-17
[253] Judges 2:16-23, I Samuel 3:19-20
[254] I Samuel 8:4-22

There are other books in the Bible that seem boring to us but are significant to all God's people. The book of **Leviticus** are laws required for sin since it was God's desire to restore all people to thrive with Him in peace. Then, when the people make a sacrifice for their sin, it renews their relationship with God through their sacrifice and helps them recognize their need for forgiveness of sin. However, these laws were only a temporary fix for sin, foreshadowing the need for Jesus, the Lamb of God, a perfect sacrifice offered for our sins, which would make a permanent way to have a relationship with God.

The book of **Numbers** is all about God's people in the wilderness, how they got there, how God dealt with them, and how God brought them out of the wilderness on their way to the Promised Land. God took the people through the wilderness to avoid them from getting killed by their enemies, but God did not intend for them to live there. God asked Moses to number the men for battle so they would be prepared to fight against their enemies when they came into the Promised Land (Canaan). It was because of the people's rebellion that God would not allow them into the Promised Land until the next generation, and then Moses would need to number the men for battle again. I believe this is a good example of people now, as they choose to be rebellious against God by rejecting the free gift of salvation, and then they cannot enter the Promised Land, which would be their permanent home in Heaven.

In the book of **Deuteronomy**, Moses exhorts the people to remember the Ten Commandments, laws, plus decrees and reminds them to teach their children also. God loves His people and needs to remind them He wants to bless them in the Promised Land, but they must be obedient. This foreshadows even the importance of obedience today because faith is nothing without obedience and God cannot bless us if we are disobedient.

219

It is hard to compare God to us as parents because He is the creator of everything and knows the beginning from the end. Although as a parent, we can relate to our Father God because we also love our children, care for them, set limits for their protection, and disciple them. The nature of our children is to sin, so that is why it is best to be strict and consistent with our disciples. This helps to build a firm foundation for right and wrong, so they know the results they reap when they disobey. When our children are secure in our love they will understand the importance of disciple. I have even heard a psychologist say that children that are undiscipline feel unloved. No matter how much we love our children they can provoke us to anger if they continue to be disobedient to us, but we should never disciple them out of anger. Since we created in God's image, we also have similarities of the same love and discipline for our children. God is as a good and loving father to all His children in the Old Testament and New Testament. It tells us in Proverbs 3:12, "For whom the LORD loves He reproves (disciplines)," even as a father, the son in whom he delights."

It is important to know God never hates us but hates the sin that makes us disobedient and causes separation in our relationship with Him.

HEALTHY RECIPES

HELPFUL TIPS WHEN PURCHASING
HEALTHY INGREDIENTS

Baking Powder - We assume it is a safe ingredient for baking, but it has aluminum in it.

Baking Soda – This can contain gluten or be genetically modified (GMO).

Cheese - When produced in a natural form it is pasteurized at the lowest heat, so the nutrients remain, and they use natural enzymes with no preservatives. This makes the cheese not only more nutritious but easier to digest. This also applies to the natural process of milk too.

Cold-Pressed Oils – These oils are extracted by crushing the seeds under pressure using low-heating methods. The process does not contain harmful chemicals or preservatives. Natural oils become rancid easily, so they pour them in dark-colored bottles to protect them from light. They also need to be refrigerated after opening to prolong the life of the oil. Since they are produced naturally that also gives you all the natural vitamins, minerals, and antioxidants that they provide. Bottles of oils at the grocery store are in clear bottles or plastic because they over process the oil with heat to be self-safe, but it does not keep the nutritional value.

Eggs – The ones you eat from your grocery store are not a healthy choice. First, you do not know what food quality the chickens are eating or how long the eggs have been sitting around before they are sold. They put the eggs through the process of washing them. This takes off the natural protection from the shell that keeps bacteria out, so there is a greater chance of getting salmonella too. The best eggs to buy are free range, which are from chickens that also get to be outside the chicken coop. I raised free range chickens on organic grains, and they were heathy, happy running around outside to eat bugs. The yolks are darker and taste much better.

Fruit - It is supposed to be healthier to eat locally grown. Even though tropical fruits have good nutritional value, most are high on the acidic pH chart, so it is best to limit the amount you consume. Also, the reality is that all fruits that come from foreign countries are irradiated (radiation) to kill off microorganisms and insects but that also removes most of the nutrients. Even locally grown fruits use pesticides if you are not eating organic fruit. It is helpful to use fruit wash to remove residue and chemicals.

Gluten - This is a protein naturally found in most grains, including wheat, barley, spelt and rye. It acts like a binder, holding food together and adding a stretchy quality. Unfortunately, people are becoming intolerant to gluten because of the overabundance of it in all processed food.

GMO – This process can be accomplished with vegetables, fruit, or animals, in which changes are made using high-tech genetic engineering in an attempt to alter the characteristics. Foods become unstable when genetically modified which cause loss of nutrient value, or cause bad health effects. Unfortunately, there is no law that says they have to reveal it is GMO with the product.

Honey is very nutritional and has considerable amounts of vitamin B. It is best to use raw honey, to avoid overly processed honey that loses nutritional value. Honey digests quickly, so a diabetic should be cautious because it can give you a sugar spike.

Hydrogenated oils – These are oils put through a chemical process which are used for making processed food to keep it fresher for longer. In the body, it increases levels of LDL (bad) cholesterol while decreasing the good HDL (good) cholesterol, which is harmful for the heart. In the body it breaks down as bad sugars that make the arteries sticky and cause blocked arteries.

Organic – This means the plants are grown without chemicals. When farming with fertilizers, pesticides, and herbicides, it depletes the soil of important minerals. When we eat the food grown in that soil, we will lack the nutrients we need.

Black Pepper – This is a spice that is hard to digest. It is best to use in moderation and in the form of a grinder of white or rainbow peppercorn.

Sprouted Grains - This means as soon as the grains have sprouted, they grind them into flour. Since they are a living food before they are ground, the enzymes are released during the process of sprouting, which breaks down proteins and carbohydrates. This process helps make it low in glycemic value and easier to digest.

Refined flour and Sugar – This is processed white flour and white sugar used in making all processed foods in bakeries, stores, and restaurants. Try to avoid these since they cause inflammation and excess fat in the body. You can look for alternative choices of flour and sugar in natural packaged food. You can also replace them with alternative choices when making your own meals and desserts.

Salt – This makes everything taste better, but as in anything, moderation is best. All refined salt is void of any natural minerals because of the processing, which is why they iodize it. When you use rock salt like Himalayan salts, you get all the benefits of the minerals, and you do not need extra iodine.

Soya – All Soy is genetically modified if not labeled as non-GMO. Women with estrogen dominance should stay away from anything with soya because it has a high concentration of Isoflavones, which is a plant source of estrogen.

Tofu – This is prepared by coagulating soy milk and then pressing the resulting curds into solid blocks of various softness. It is high in protein and an alternative to dairy. You can add tofu to any recipe, and it takes on the flavor of the recipe. I use it as a dairy alternative in lasagna, and no one has noticed. You can get non-GMO Tofu at the Health Food Store.

You can make any of your favorite recipes healthier by replacing ingredients with natural alternatives.

If you do eat meat or add it to your recipes it is always better for you to use organic or naturally raised animals. Caution: With fish make sure it is not from China because of the bacteria build up in packing and shipping. Also avoid farmed fish because of toxin build up in the confined water area where they are raised. Wild caught and cold-water fish are the best choice because they are healthy fish.

BREAKFAST

BANANA-QUINOA BREAKFAST BARS

BANANA-QUINOA BREAKFAST BARS

Quinoa is an excellent source of protein, fiber, vitamins, and minerals. It is an excellent addition to salads and main dishes, but it can also be used in baking.

Ingredients:

- 1 1/2 cups organic GF oats
- 1 cup cooked organic quinoa
- 1/3 cup cane sugar
- 1 teaspoon aluminum-free baking powder
- 1 heaping teaspoon organic cinnamon
- 1/2 teaspoon organic nutmeg
- 1/2 teaspoon Himalayan salt
- 2 free-range eggs
- 1 cup mashed bananas (2 med.)
- 1 teaspoon organic vanilla extract
- 1/4 cup organic nut butter of your choice

Directions:

Preheat oven to 350°F. Line an 8×8 baking pan with parchment paper and grease.

In a large mixing bowl, whisk together the oats, quinoa, sugar, baking powder, spices, and salt. In a separate bowl, mix the banana, vanilla, and nut butter together. Then, stir in the eggs and pour this mixture over the dry ingredients, mixing everything together until fully mixed. The batter should be moist but not runny. Pour the batter into the prepared pan and smooth with a spatula.

Bake on the center rack for 15-20 minutes until the bars are golden brown and solid to the touch. Allow it to cool, and then cut.

CORN BREAD MUFFINS OR LOAF

CORN BREAD MUFFINS OR LOAF

This recipe is a family favorite at our Sunday night dinners or with soup. It is one that I have made for many years, and it is a great add-on to any meal. I modified my original recipe by using Pamela's gluten-free flour and the taste is just as good. You can make this simple change to any number of your all-time favorite bread and dessert recipes to make them gluten-free.

Ingredients

- 1 cup organic stone ground cornmeal
- 1 cup Pamela's GF flour
- 4 teaspoons alum-free baking powder
- ½ teaspoon Himalayan salt
- 2 tablespoons organic cane sugar
- ¼ cup raw coconut oil (solid)
- 1 cup non-dairy milk
- 1 egg

Directions

Heat oven to 425f. Grease the bottoms of 12 medium muffin tin or use paper liners. If you prefer a loaf pour batter in a Wilton 9" loaf tin.

Blend dry ingredients together with a fork. Blend cane sugar and coconut oil with a fork, then add to the corn mixture. Beat the egg into milk, slowly add it to the corn mixture, and mix it all together for about 20 seconds, just enough to blend it together.

Fill the muffin cups 2/3 full and bake for 15 minutes. Take out of the oven and butter the tops of all muffins while hot. With a toothpick, put holes all around the top of the muffins and pour maple syrup on top. This gives the cornbread more moisture and flavor. Take them out of the tin to put in a serving basket and serve them warm.

HEALTHIER OATMEAL CHOICE

HEALTHIER OATMEAL CHOICE

My husband wanted a different option than oatmeal, so I came up with this recipe. I usually like to use steel-cut oats because no processing is done to the grain, but some people like the rolled flake version. So, I added a bit of both and some other ingredients to make it even healthier. This oatmeal is also full of extra fiber, omega oils, and protein. Since oats are a carbohydrate, cinnamon helps to balance the sugars.

Ingredients

- 3 cups of purified water
- ¾ teaspoon Himalayan salt
- ¾ cup organic steel-cut oats
- ¼ cup organic sprouted grain oat flakes
- 1 tablespoon flax
- 1 tablespoon hemp hearts
- ¼ teaspoon cinnamon

*Option - instead, use ½ cup steel cut oats, ¼ oat flakes and ¼ quinoa

Directions

In a medium-sized pan, put cold purified water then add the salt, steel-cut oats, sprouted oat flakes, and quinoa. On medium-high heat, boil the mixture and skim off all white foam as it cooks till it is gone. After it cooks for about ½ hour, add other ingredients, stir, cover, and let it cook itself for 30 to 60 minutes. It will thicken by itself while sitting. I like to do that and come back as I get ready for church. You can reheat it if you need to and then put it in your bowls. I add raisins or whatever fruit you like and sprinkle with cinnamon.

MUSHROOM SPINACH FRITTATA

MUSHROOM SPINACH FRITTATA

Ingredients

- 10 organic eggs or free-range
- 1/3 cup almond milk or another dairy-free beverage
- ¾ teaspoon Himalayan salt and fresh ground pepper to taste
- ½ cup grated natural parmesan cheese
- 2 tablespoons cold pressed olive oil
- 1 small organic red onion
- 2 cloves garlic minced
- ½ organic red pepper
- 1 cup fresh mushrooms, sliced
- 1 cup organic spinach leaves, chopped

Directions

Preheat the oven to 400 F.

In a medium bowl, whisk together eggs and milk until egg whites and yolks are blended with milk. Then whisk in salt, fresh ground pepper, and parmesan cheese and set aside. In a 10-inch oven-safe skillet, heat the olive oil over medium heat. Sauté the onions, garlic, mushrooms, and red pepper until they are soft, and the mushrooms brown (about 5 minutes). Add the spinach and sauté for another minute. Pour the egg mixture into the skillet and make sure the spinach and mushrooms are arranged evenly.

Cook for about 5 to 7 minutes over medium heat until the bottom is set, and then sprinkle the top with a little more parmesan. Place the skillet in the oven and bake for 10-15 minutes when the top puffs up and slightly brown. Cool for 5 minutes, cut into wedges, and serve warm.

SWEET POTATO, EGG AND TOFU SQUARES

SWEET POTATO, EGG AND TOFU SQUARES

This recipe is packed with protein, which is great for any meal. You can also add sprouted grain toast, cut-up fruit, or veggies to go along with it.

Ingredients:

- 6 organic eggs
- ½ package non-GMO soft tofu
- 3 sun-dried tomatoes packed in oil, chopped
- 1 tsp Himalayan salt and add pepper to taste
- 1 large organic sweet potato, cooked, peeled, and chopped
- ½ organic red pepper, chopped
- 1 cup chopped organic broccoli florets
- ¾ cup crumbled feta

Directions:

Preheat oven to 350°F.

Crack eggs into a large bowl, crumble in tofu, and add salt. Using a hand blender, whirl until well mixed. Fold sweet potato, red pepper, sun-dried tomatoes, and broccoli.

Pour into an 8-inch square baking dish lined with parchment paper. Sprinkle with cheese, and then bake until the eggs are set 35 to 40 minutes. Let stand for 5 minutes, and then cut into squares.

VEGGIE EGGS

VEGGIE EGGS

When I was not sure what to make for dinner one night, this is what recipe I made up. It turned out to be delicious and nutritious. It is so easy to make because you can put any vegetable in it you have and make it for any meal. The idea is more veggies than eggs!

Ingredients – These are the veggies I added that are in the picture.

- 2 tablespoons cold pressed avocado oil
- organic small red potatoes cut up in small wedge pieces
- organic asparagus
- organic zucchini
- organic red pepper
- organic spinach, chopped
- garlic granules, salt, and pepper to taste
- 1 organic or free-range egg per person

Directions

Add oil to a medium size fry pan and put on a medium temperature. Then add cut potatoes, onion, garlic, salt, pepper and cook till potatoes are almost soft. Lower heat to medium, add all other veggies and cook till almost done. Add spinach for just a few minutes. In a small bowl beat the eggs with a fork till it is completely mixed and add a bit of salt and pepper to the egg mix. Pour it over top of veggies and let cook for 5 minutes and flip it over in sections to cook the other side for 5 minutes. Make sure the egg mixture is equally distributed so there is a bit of egg through all the veggie mixture. Place on warm plates, drizzle with a bit of ketchup or salsa and shave a bit of cheddar cheese on the top.

You can serve it with toast for breakfast. If you make it for lunch or dinner you can spice it up with a bit of salsa on top and tortillas around the sides of the plate.

GLUTEN-FREE PANCAKES OR WAFFLES

GLUTEN-FREE PANCAKES OR WAFFLES

This recipe is a meal in one, with protein, fiber, antioxidants, and omega oils. They are fluffy and delicious.

Ingredients:

- 1 ½ cups Pamela's GF Artisan Flour Blend
- 2 teaspoon Aluminum free baking powder
- 1 teaspoon GF baking soda
- ¾ teaspoon Himalayan salt
- 1 cup plus 2 tablespoons almond milk
- 1 tablespoon apple cider vinegar
- 2 tablespoon agave or organic sugar
- 2 tablespoons coconut oil, melted
- 2 free range eggs, large
- **Optional Additions:**
- 3 tablespoons ground walnuts or pecans
- ½ tsp organic vanilla extract
- ¼ tsp organic cinnamon
- 1 -2 Tablespoons hemp hearts
- add banana to mixture
- blueberries

You can use all of these options or choose what options you want. You may need to add more liquid because of the hemp hearts.

Directions:

Mix dry ingredients together. In a separate bowl, mix the liquid ingredients. Whisk together the wet and dry ingredients and use the batter immediately. The batter thickens as it sits, add more milk to thin as needed.

LUNCH

BLACK BEAN VEGGIE BURGERS

BLACK BEAN VEGGIE BURGERS

These burgers are so easy to make and a hit with my family and friends. They are my favorite veggie burgers because they taste great and do not fall apart on the BBQ like most veggie burgers. I make them ahead, put them in fridge and take them to summer BBQ's on our boat.

Ingredients

- 1 (16 ounce) can organic black beans, drained and rinsed
- ½ organic red bell pepper, cut into 2-inch pieces
- ½ small organic red onion, chopped
- 3 garlic cloves, chopped
- 1 free range egg
- 1 teaspoon chili powder
- 1 teaspoon cumin
- 1 teaspoon salsa
- 1 cup sprouted grain oats
- ½ teaspoon salt and grind pepper corns

Recipe makes 4 burgers

Directions

Mash black beans in a medium bowl with a fork until thick and pasty.

Place bell pepper, onion, and garlic in food processor and then stir chopped vegetables into mashed beans.

Stir together egg, chili powder, cumin, and taco sauce in a small bowl. Add to the mashed bean mixture and stir to combine. Mix in oatmeal until the mixture is sticky and holds together. Divide the mixture into four patties. To make ahead put natural wax paper between patties and put in container to keep in fridge till BBQ. If you need more burgers, double the recipe.

I put directly on a heated grill for about 8 minutes on each side. You can also lightly oil a sheet of foil on top the grill to cook. I serve them with humus spread on the sprouted grain bun, then add tomato and lettuce.

*You can also add more spices if you like them to be spicier.

BLACK BEAN AND QUINOA
ENCHILADA BAKE

BLACK BEAN AND QUINOA
ENCHILADA BAKE

This recipe is a new favorite at our house and a wonderful change to our regular taco night.

Ingredients:

- 1 cup uncooked organic quinoa, rinsed
- 2 cups water
- 1 tablespoon cold pressed olive oil
- 1 small organic onion, diced
- 3 cloves organic garlic, minced
- 1 organic red pepper, remove seeds, dice
- 1 orange pepper, remove seeds, dice
- 1 cup frozen corn kernels
- juice of 1 small lime
- 1 teaspoon ground cumin
- 1 tablespoon chili powder
- 1/3 cup chopped fresh organic cilantro
- salt and pepper, to taste
- 2 cans of black beans, drained, and rinsed
- 2 cups taco sauce or salsa
- 2 cups shredded organic cheddar cheese

Toppings: Sliced green onions, avocado slices, sour cream

Directions:
Preheat oven to 350° F. Grease a 9×13 baking dish with cooking spray and set aside.

Add quinoa to water in a medium saucepan and bring to a boil over medium-high heat. Boil for 5 minutes. Turn the heat to low and simmer for about 15 minutes or until water absorbs. Remove from heat and fluff with a fork. Cover quinoa and set aside.

In a large skillet, heat the tablespoon of olive oil over medium-high heat. Add the onion, garlic and red pepper. Sauté until softened, for about 5 minutes. Add the corn. Cook for about 3-4 minutes. Add lime juice, cumin, chili powder, and cilantro. Stir to combine. Season with salt and pepper, to taste.

In a large bowl, add the cooked quinoa and black beans. Add the sautéed vegetable mixture and stir to combine. Pour in the taco sauce and stir. Add ½ cup of shredded cheese. If you want to limit your cheese intake like I do, you can add just half the amount of cheese.

Pour the black bean and quinoa mixture into the prepared baking dish. Top with remaining shredded cheese. Cover the dish with foil. Bake for 20 minutes, then remove foil. Bake an additional 10 minutes, or until the cheese is melted and edges are bubbling. Remove from the oven, and let cool for 10 minutes. Fill the enchiladas and serve.

CABBAGE, CARROT AND APPLE SALAD

CABBAGE, CARROT AND APPLE SALAD

If you are looking for a simple salad to add to any meal, then this one is perfect.

Ingredients:

- ½ small organic red or white cabbage (can buy an organic blend of both pre sliced at health food store)
- 2 organic carrots, grated
- 2 organic apples, grated
- ¼ cup cranberries
- ¼ cup chopped pecans
- 2 Tablespoons natural mayonnaise or yogurt
- ½ lemon, squeezed
- ½ teaspoon organic sugar

*option sprinkle of Himalayan salt

Directions:

Grate up cabbage plus cut some into smaller pieces. Shave the carrot to grate into the cabbage, core apple and shred with the peel on, and then add pecans and cranberries. Mix lemon, mayonnaise, and sugar then blend into the cabbage mixture.

EVERYTHING HEALTHY BOWL

EVERYTHING HEALTHY BOWL

This bowl is a simple meal for lunch, hot or cold! You can also make extra to put in containers for more lunches.

Ingredients:

- 1 cup organic quinoa (white or mixed)
- 2 cups water
- 2 teaspoons cold pressed extra-virgin olive oil
- ¼ cup pesto (You can buy it prepared or make it from fresh basil or spinach)
- 1/3 cup roughly chopped raw walnuts
- 1-15 oz. can organic chickpeas, drained and rinsed
- ½ cup chopped organic artichoke hearts
- 1 yellow pepper, diced
- 1 cup halved grape cherry tomatoes cut in half

Directions:

Put water in a medium sized pot and add quinoa. Bring to boil, reduce heat to low and let simmer until water absorbs, about 15 minutes. Remove from heat, fluff with fork, and set aside to cool.

Meanwhile, combine olive oil and pesto and stir to combine. When quinoa is still warm or you can let it cool, add pesto to quinoa and gently combine until pesto is evenly distributed. Add the remaining ingredients and toss to combine. Split among 4 bowls and serve, or among 4 airtight containers and refrigerate.

KALE AND RED CABBAGE WITH STRAWBERRIES

KALE AND RED CABBAGE WITH STRAWBERRIES

Kale is one of the most nutritious foods available. It is loaded with antioxidants and vitamin C. Using kale instead of lettuce is an effortless way to ensure you are getting the daily fiber and nutrients you need with a delicious crisp taste. To complete your lunch, add a corn muffin.

Ingredients:

- 5-6 ounces organic kale (5 cups or as needed)
- 3 cups chopped organic red cabbage
- ½ cup nuts (walnut or pecan)
- 1 ½ cup sliced organic strawberries
- ½ small organic red onion thinly slice

*Optional ½ cup crumbled feta cheese on top

Instructions:

Wash and dry kale and cut the stems off or buy container prewashed. Cut or shave the red cabbage. Toss all ingredients in a bowl. You can add dressing to individual servings.

Single Batch Dressing:

- 2 tablespoons keto oil blend (or your choice oil)
- 1 tablespoon apple cider vinegar
- 1 ½ teaspoon maple syrup
- ¼ teaspoon Braggs liquid seasoning

Big Batch Dressing:

- 2/3 cup oil
- ½ cup apple cider vinegar
- 2 tablespoons maple syrup
- 1 teaspoon Braggs liquid seasoning

MEXICAN CHEF SALAD

MEXICAN CHEF SALAD

This is anytime favorite recipe I've been making for years. This recipe can be made with all options added or just the ones you like. I always prefer to add other dark greens too. You can double the recipe when needed.

Ingredients:

- Package of pre-washed organic Romaine lettuce
- ½ can organic black beans 398 ml
- ½ bag organic frozen corn 350 g
- Organic tomatoes cut up or cherry tomatoes cut in half
- Tortillas
- Organic cheddar cheese (amount desired)

Directions:

Place all the lettuce in a large salad bowl. Rinse and drain beans, thaw out corn in convection oven, and cut up tomatoes. Then add them to lettuce mixture with salad forks. Shave cheese, break up tortillas and mix into lettuce mixture with salad forks. Place the salad in bowls, top with more broken tortillas plus grate more cheese on top, then serve. Makes 4 bowls

*Other options: add spinach or kale to add dark greens, cut pieces of avocado and for meat lovers, seasoned ground beef.

Recipe for French Salad Dressing – Add whatever dressing you like but our favorite is homemade French dressing to top off the Mexican salad.

- ¾ cold pressed avocado oil
- 1 teaspoon lemon juice
- ½ cup organic ketchup
- ½ teaspoon paprika
- 1/3 cup cane sugar
- ¼ teaspoon salt
- ¼ cup apple cider vinegar
- onion diced into small pieces

Mix all together by stirring well. Place the dressing in 350 glass salad dressing bottle and shake well each time before use it, so it doesn't separate. Place leftover dressing in the fridge for other salads.

AVOCADO EGG WRAP

AVOCADO EGG WRAP

This is another recipe I made to give us another healthy option for lunch. My husband loves them!

Ingredients:

- Small, sprouted grain spinach wraps (can use multi grain or use larger wraps)
- 1 avocado, soft (add more if you are using more than 2 eggs)
- 1 egg per wrap (larger wrap at least 2 eggs each)
- Hummus
- Spinach as per needed
- Tomatoes as per needed
- Salt and pepper to taste

Directions:

Fill a pot with cold water, place eggs in and bring to a boil. After it boils tun off heat, cover and let set for 10 minutes. Then dump hot water, put cold water in the pan with eggs and let it set for a few minutes. That should help you to get the shells off the egg easier and you can run under cold water as peel.

Cut the eggs in small pieces in a bowl. Cut the avocado in half and pull it apart to get seed out. Scrape out the insides of avocado into the eggs. With a fork (or hand masher) mash the egg and avocado together to make creamy. Cut up spinach, tomato and add to the avocado mixture. Then add salt and pepper and mix together.

Lay the wraps flat and spread with hummus. Fill with egg mixture and wrap.

Options: add kale instead of spinach, onion, salsa

DINNER

CHICKPEA SOUP

CHICKPEA SOUP

I love soup to warm up with for lunch or dinner in the winter. This is one of my favorite soup recipes because it taste great, and it is simple to make.

Ingredients:

- 2 tablespoons virgin olive oil
- ¼ teaspoon paprika
- 1 small organic onion, chopped
- 1 tomato, chopped
- 2 cloves garlic, minced
- 1 (10 ounce) pack frozen mixed vegetables
- 2 cups peeled, cubed sweet potato
- 1 can chickpeas, drained
- 3 cups organic vegetable broth
- ½ -1 teaspoon salt
- 1 bay leaf
- ground black pepper to taste
- 1 teaspoon dried basil

Directions:

In a large soup pan, warm oil over moderate heat. Add onion, garlic, and sweet potatoes and sauté 5 minutes.

Stir in broth, bay leaf, and paprika. Bring to boil, and then reduce heat to medium low. Cover and simmer until vegetables are tender but not mushy, about 15 minutes.

Stir in tomato, mixed vegetables, and chickpeas. Simmer until tender, about 10 minutes more. Serve hot!

CREAMY CAULIFLOWER AND PARNIP
SOUP

CREAMY CAULIFLOWER AND PARNIP
SOUP

Ingredients:

- 1 tablespoon organic butter
- 1 teaspoon Himalayan salt
- 2 cloves garlic, thinly sliced
- 1 teaspoon dried basil
- 1 medium onion, coarsely chopped
- 3 parsnips peeled and thinly sliced
- 2 ½ cups rice milk, more for desired thinning
- 1 head cauliflower, florets
- 2 tablespoons organic long-grain rice
- optional garnish: cinnamon, nuts

Directions:

Heat on low heat, the butter and oil in a soup pot. Add the garlic and onions and cook, stirring frequently until the onions are soft and translucent, about 10 minutes.

Add the milk, 1 cup water, rice, salt, basil, parsnips, and cauliflower. Bring to a boil, and then reduce to a simmer, cover, and cook until the cauliflower and parsnips are tender, and the rice is thoroughly cooked, about 15 minutes. Do not be surprised if the milk looks curled, it will become creamy once it is pureed.

Get a hand blender to puree it in the pot. Then garnish and serve.

PESTO PENNE PRIMAVERA

PESTO PENNE PRIMAVERA

Ingredients:

- 1 cup fresh organic basil leaves (can substitute spinach for basil)
- 2 cloves minced garlic
- ½ cup pine nuts
- 1 cup organic parmesan cheese
- 1/4 cup cold pressed olive oil
- 2 tablespoons squeezed lemon juice
- 4 cups brown rice penne pasta
- 2 tablespoons cold pressed olive oil
- 1 cup chopped organic asparagus
- ½ cup chopped organic zucchini
- ½ cup sliced kalamata (black) olives
- ½ cup diced organic red pepper
- ½ cup chopped sun-dried tomatoes

Directions:

Combine the basil, garlic and 1/4 cup pine nuts, 1/2 cup Parmesan cheese, 1/4 cup olive oil, and lemon juice in a food processor and blend until well combined and has the texture of fresh pesto and set aside.

Bring a pot of lightly salted water to boil. Cook the pasta in boiling water until cooked yet firm to the bite, about 8 minutes. Drain the pasta and transfer to a large bowl. Pour 1 tablespoon of oil over the pasta and toss to coat and set aside.

Heat 1 tablespoon of olive oil in a large skillet over medium heat. Roast the pine nuts in the skillet until lightly browned then add the asparagus, zucchini, Kalamata olives, red pepper, and sun-dried tomatoes to the skillet, then cook and stir until hot, 5-7 minutes. Add the pesto to the pasta, and toss to combine. Serve in bowls topped with grated parmesan or feta cheese.

STUFFED PEPPER WITH QUINOA AND CHICKPEAS

STUFFED PEPPER WITH QUINOA AND CHICKPEAS

Ingredients:

- 1 teaspoon cold pressed olive oil
- 1 1/3 cups water
- 2/3 cup organic quinoa
- 1 (16 ounce) can organic chickpeas beans, drained and rinsed
- 1 (16 ounce) tomato sauce or spaghetti sauce
- ¼ cup walnut pieces, chopped
- ½ cup raisins
- 1 small onion, diced
- ½ lemon, juiced
- ½ teaspoon chili powder
- ¼ teaspoon garlic powder
- 1/8 teaspoon ground cinnamon
- 2 large bell peppers, halved lengthwise, seeds and pepper membrane removed
- ¼ cup crumbled goat cheese or parmesan cheese

Directions:

Preheat oven to 350° F. Grease a 9×13-inch baking dish with olive oil.

Bring water, oil, and quinoa boil in a saucepan. Reduce heat to low, cover, and simmer until quinoa is tender and water absorbs, 15 to 20 minutes. Mix garbanzo beans, walnuts, raisins, onions, lemon juice, chili powder, garlic powder, cinnamon, and tomato sauce together in a bowl; stir in cooked quinoa.

Arrange the pepper halves, facing upwards, in the prepared glass dish. Put a small amount of water in the bottom of the baking dish. Spoon quinoa mixture into each bell pepper. Bake in preheated oven until bell peppers are tender, about 30 minutes. Top each with 1 tablespoon goat cheese or parmesan.

SWEET POTATO, BROCCOLI, AND CHICKEN BAKE

SWEET POTATO, BROCCOLI, AND CHICKEN BAKE

The family loves this dinner, and you can serve it with cabbage, carrot, and apple salad. It is easy to make for guests too. You can make it without the chicken for vegetarians. I don't make meat very often but I do like chicken occasionally, especially this recipe.

Ingredients:

- 2 boneless, skinless organic chicken breasts cubed
- 3 cups packed organic broccoli stems and florets, chopped.
- 1 large, organic sweet potato, ¼ inch small cubes
- 1/2 red onion, chopped
- 2 cloves garlic, minced
- 3 tablespoons raisins
- 2 tablespoons chopped walnuts
- 1/3 cup cold pressed virgin olive oil
- 1 ½ tsp basil (dried)
- ½ tsp Himalayan salt
- ¼ teaspoon pepper (ground fresh)
- ¼ cup soft goat feta cheese, crumbled on top (optional)

Directions:

Preheat oven to 375°F. Grease a large casserole dish with olive oil. Place cubed chicken on the bottom of the casserole dish. Lightly season with salt and pepper. In a bowl combine broccoli, sweet potatoes, red onion, garlic, raisins, chopped walnuts, olive oil and herbs. Toss to coat. Top the chicken with herb, and vegetable mixture. Cover and bake for 35 minutes. Remove the cover and bake for an additional 10-15 minutes or until chicken is no longer pink and the sweet potatoes are soft. Top with optional cheese just before serving.

SWEET POTATO, CARROT, APPLE, AND RED LENTIL SOUP

SWEET POTATO, CARROT, APPLE, AND RED LENTIL SOUP

This soup is perfect for those cold days. It is high in fiber, protein, and packed full of nutrients, with a nice thick creamy texture to stick to your ribs. Even my husband is a huge fan of this hearty soup! Also serve with corn bread.

Ingredients:

- ¼ cup raw organic coconut oil
- ½ teaspoon ground black pepper
- 2 large organic sweet potatoes, peeled and chopped
- 1 teaspoon Himalayan salt
- 3 large organic carrots, peeled and chopped
- ½ teaspoon ground cumin
- 1 organic apple peeled, cored and chopped
- ½ teaspoon chili powder
- ½ small organic onion, chopped
- ½ teaspoon paprika
- ½ cup red lentils
- 4 cups vegetable broth

Directions:

Melt the coconut oil in a large pot over medium heat. Place the chopped sweet potatoes, carrot, apple, and onion in the pot. Stir and cook the apples and vegetables until the onions are translucent, about 10 minutes.

Stir in lentils, ground pepper, salt, cumin, chili powder, paprika, and vegetable broth in the pot with the apple and vegetable mixture. Bring the soup to boil over high heat, then reduce the heat to medium low, cover, and simmer until the lentils are soft, about 30 minutes.

Use a handheld potato masher to get the ingredients to a mashed consistency. Then get a handheld blender to puree the mixture to a nice thick consistency. Bring back to a simmer over low to medium heat for about 10 minutes. You can garnish with a spoon full of yogurt or hummus and sprinkle with cinnamon.

TOMATO-BASIL PASTA

TOMATO-BASIL PASTA

Ingredients:

- 9 ounces brown rice pasta
- 1 teaspoon cold pressed extra-virgin olive oil
- 1 small onion, diced
- 2 cloves garlic, minced
- 2 ½ cups diced fresh or canned organic tomatoes (drain juice for canned)
- 3 handfuls organic spinach, chopped
- ½ cup cashew milk (or other nondairy milk)
- ¼ cup grated L'Ancetre artisan goat cheese (or parmesan cheese)
- 1 cup packed fresh basil, finely chopped
- 3 tablespoons tomato paste
- 1 teaspoon dried organic oregano
- 1 teaspoon fine-grain Himalayan salt, or to taste
- ¼ teaspoon freshly ground black pepper, or to taste

Directions:

Bring a large pot of salted water to a boil. Cook the pasta for about 8 minutes.

In a large pan heat the oil over medium heat. Add the onion and garlic and sauté for 5 to 10 minutes, or until the onion is translucent. Add the diced tomatoes and spinach and continue cooking for 7 to 10 minutes over medium heat, until the spinach wilts.

Stir in the cashew milk, cheese, basil, tomato paste, oregano, salt, and pepper, and cook for 5 to 10 minutes more, or until heated through.

Drain the pasta and add it to the pan and stir to combine the pasta with the sauce. Cook for a few minutes, or until heated through. Season with extra salt and pepper to taste and serve immediately. Before served you can also add more fresh basil, cheese and chopped cashews on top of each serving.

DESSERTS

SIMPLE APPLE CRISP

SIMPLE APPLE CRISP

Over the Thanksgiving weekend one year our family was busy with the usual traditions of pumpkin racing, ATV rides and a delicious dinner. No Thanksgiving dinner is complete without dessert and that year we were treated to a delicious apple crisp that my son made. He used the apples we pick as a family from a local organic orchard near our home.

Ingredients:

- 6 organic apples
- 1 cup organic brown sugar
- 1 teaspoon organic vanilla extract
- ¾ cup uncooked (gluten-free) oats
- ½ cup Pamela's (gluten-free) flour
- 1 teaspoon organic cinnamon
- ½ organic butter (cold)

Directions:

Preheat oven to 350° F. Peel, core and slice the apples. You can leave the apples plain or sprinkle them with a little bit of cinnamon and sugar. In a medium bowl combine brown sugar, vanilla, oats, flour, and cinnamon. Use a pastry blender to cut in the cold butter. When the mixture looks nice and crumbly you can place it on top of the apples. Bake for 30-35 minutes or until the topping is browned and apples are soft. Taste even better with organic vanilla ice cream on top!

BANANA BLUEBERRY MUFFINS

BANANA BLUEBERRY MUFFINS

Ingredients:

- 3 large very ripe bananas
- ¾ cup organic cane sugar
- 1 organic or free-range egg, slightly beaten
- 1/3 cup organic virgin coconut oil
- 1 cup fresh blueberries
- 1 teaspoon non-GMO baking soda
- 1 teaspoon alum-free baking powder
- ½ teaspoon Himalayan salt
- 1 ½ cups Pamela's Gluten-Free flour
- ½ cup dark chocolate chips

Directions:

Mash the bananas in a large mixing bowl to set aside.

Add the sugar, egg, and coconut oil together.

Combine the dry ingredients to sugar mixture, then blend in mashed banana.

Fold in the blueberries.

Pour into 12 well-greased muffin cups

Bake at 375°F for 20 minutes

BLUEBERRY GOAT CHEESE TART

BLUEBERRY GOAT CHEESE TART

This is a delicious recipe I found and made modifications to make it healthier. I wanted to try it, so my daughter in law made it for a family meal. I love cheesecake and it was a big hit with everyone in the family. It was a delicious dessert that was neither heavy nor too sweet.

Ingredients:

Crust

- ¾ cup organic almond flour
- ½ cup Pamela's gluten-free flour
- ½ teaspoon ground flax
- 1/3 cup packed brown sugar
- 3 tablespoons melted grass feed butter
- 1 large free-range egg, lightly beaten

Filling

- 4 oz (125g) soft unripen goat cheese
- ¾ cup plain Greek yogurt
- 3 tablespoons raw honey
- ½ teaspoon pure vanilla extract

Sauce

- 3 tablespoons raw liquid honey
- 2 ½ teaspoons tapioca flour or non-GMO cornstarch
- 1 ¾ cups thawed frozen blueberries

Directions:

For the crust, whisk together the almond and gluten-free flours and ground flax. Using a wooden spoon, stir in the sugar and then work in the butter, using clean hands for this stage if necessary. Stir in the egg white until fully combined. Press into the prepared tart pan. Bake for 12 minutes in a 350°F oven. Remove from the oven and cool completely.

For the filling, place the goat cheese, yogurt, honey, and vanilla in a medium mixing bowl. Use a handheld mixer to mix everything fully. Spread the filling evenly over the cooled crust. Cool in the refrigerator for 45 minutes.

For the sauce, whisk the honey and tapioca flour in a medium saucepan with 1/3 cup of water. Add the thawed blueberries. Warm the berry mixture over medium-low heat, stirring frequently until the sauce has come to a boil. Let it boil for 1 minute, until it thickens enough to coat the back of a spoon.

Allow the sauce to cool to room temperature, then spread evenly over the goat cheese filling, distributing the berries equally across the top. Cool in the refrigerator for at least 1 hour before removing from the pan and cutting into 12 slices.

CRISY RICE SQUARES

CRISY RICE SQUARES

These are a great hit with our grandchildren and a much healthier choice!

Ingredients:

- ½ cup fresh ground almond butter (or any nut butter)
- ½ cup maple syrup
- ¼ teaspoon spoon Himalayan salt
- 1 tsp pure vanilla extract
- 3 cups natural crisp rice cereal (Natures Path)
- ¾ hemp hearts
- 1 ½ cup dark chocolate chips

Directions:

In a pot over medium heat, combine almond butter, maple syrup, and sea salt. Stir until warm and melts together. Stir in vanilla, and then add warm mixture to rice and hempseed. Once mixed add chocolate chips and fold in quickly so they do not completely melt. Transfer to an 8 x 8 greased pan and press evenly. Refrigerate until cool, cut into squares and serve.

FRESH CRANBERRY CAKE

FRESH CRANBERRY CAKE

This cake looks and taste delicious. It is so moist and makes a great cake to serve around Christmas.

Ingredients

- 2 cups Pamela's GF flour
- 1 teaspoon aluminum free baking soda
- 1 teaspoon salt (Himalaya)
- 1 cup organic sugar
- 3 tablespoons organic virgin coconut oil
- 2 free range eggs
- 1 cup almond milk (dairy free options)
- 3 cups fresh cranberries
- Frozen coconut whip cream

Directions

Preheat oven to 350 degrees F (175 degrees C). Grease a 9×13-inch baking dish.

Combine flour, baking soda, and salt in a bowl to set aside. Mix 1 cup sugar and 3 tablespoons coconut oil until well mixed. Then whisk the eggs into the sugar mixture. Stir milk into sugar and egg mixture until well blended and then gradually add flour mixture into that. After blending, fold cranberries into batter and pour into prepared baking dish.

Bake in the preheated oven until a toothpick inserted into the center comes out clean, about 30 minutes.

Cool completely on a wire rack.

Serve with Coconut Whip Cream on top. Place a thawed or frozen scoop on top each piece.

JOY BALLS

JOY BALLS

I had a recipe years ago like this, but lost it so I made up my own recipe. My children and grandchildren love them too! I make this recipe all the time and everywhere they go everyone wants the recipe. The wonderful thing about Joy Balls are they are a healthy sweet treat!

Ingredients

- 1 cup fresh ground almond butter
- ¼ cup raw honey or maple syrup
- ¼ cup organic pumpkin seed (raw pepitas)
- ¼ cup organic sunflower seeds
- 1/8 cup hemp hearts
- 1/8 cup raisins
- Fine unsweetened coconut

Directions

Get a small Rubbermaid or Tupperware container and line with parchment paper.

In a separate small bowl set aside the coconut. In a medium bowl cream almond butter and honey together. Then mix by hand into the almond butter each ingredient one at a time so mixes together well.

Make sure you wash your hands well before roll into balls. Get a teaspoon full of mix and roll it into a small ball in your hands. Then in the small bowl of coconut flakes, roll the balls to cover completely with coconut. Then place each ball as you make them place into the container. Makes 12 small balls and you can double the recipe if you need more.

RHUBARB CAKE

RHUBARB CAKE

This is one of my favorite desserts. I prefer to use my fresh rhubarb from the garden rather than the rhubarb I freeze, because the texture changes when using frozen rhubarb and sometimes you need to adjust the other liquid.

Ingredients:

- ½ cup organic butter or raw organic coconut oil
- 1 ½ cups cane sugar
- 1 free range egg
- 1 teaspoon organic vanilla extract
- 2 cups Pamela's GF flour
- 1 teaspoon non-GMO baking soda
- ¼ teaspoon Himalayan salt
- 1 cup nondairy milk
- 1 tablespoon apple cider vinegar
- 2 cups fresh rhubarb, chopped
- 1 tablespoon Pamela's flour

Topping

- ¼ cup organic butter or raw organic coconut oil
- 2 teaspoons organic ground cinnamon
- 1 cup packed organic brown sugar

Directions:

In a large bowl, cream together ½ cup butter and sugar. Beat in the egg and vanilla. In another bowl, sift together 2 cups flour, soda, and salt. Add sifted ingredients alternately with milk and vinegar mix to creamed mixture. Toss the rhubarb with 1 tablespoon flour and stir into batter. Spoon the batter into a buttered 9×13-inch pan, and smooth along the bottom surface.

Blend together ¼ cup butter, cinnamon, and brown sugar. Sprinkle this mixture over the top of the cake and, using a knife, gently pull it through the batter but do not blend completely.

Bake in a 350° oven for 45 minutes.

Manufactured by Amazon.ca
Bolton, ON

42355449R00164